KINGDOM JOURNEY

A MODERN DAY PILGRIM'S PROGRESS

DICK BERNAL

with
Dan & Katie Montgomery

Foreword by Ron Kenoly

Published by
Jubilee Christian Center
175 Nortech Parkway
San Jose, California 95134

Forward

For over ten years I have worked closely with my pastor, Dick Bernal. I have experienced joy and tremendous learning in submitting to his pastoral covering.

Pastor Dick is a man who is willing to courageously do God's will at the cost of friendships, reputation, or social opinion. I have stood next to him in hard times—the stress of building programs, negative press, family problems, and unethical behavior of trusted church personnel. I have seen him bend, but never seen him broken or without hope. A few times it appeared that he wanted to throw in the towel. Yet somehow he always managed to make it to the next round and keep on fighting.

Pastor Dick is man enough to admit when he is wrong, sensitive enough to share grief, quick to comfort those in need, ready to dance with those who rejoice. He is bold enough to confront foolishness, willing to give you the shirt off his back, always prepared to tell a funny story, trusting in the face of great risk, and one of the biggest name droppers I know.

Proverbs tells us that a people without a vision will perish. Pastors Dick and Carla are visionaries. Through years of obstacles I've watched them plant and replant the vision for Jubilee Christian Center. There have been many who have tried to discredit their methods and motives; but by the Holy Spirit's power they have held steady with a vision of bringing the king-

dom of God to local folks and spreading the gospel internation-
ally.

As you read Dick's life story you will laugh, cry, rejoice,
and experience the passion of a man who was a reluctant recruit
in the army of the Lord. But in spite of his admitted weaknesses
and shortcomings, Dick has become one of the leading authori-
ties on spiritual warfare and church growth.

I am convinced in my heart that because of his pastoral
love, council, and friendship, my ministry in the Lord has been
blessed and enhanced. As I travel the world, anointed, appointed, and sent out as an ambassador of praise, I am always
proud to name Jubilee Christian Center as my home church, and
Dick and Carla Bernal as my pastors. I will always love and
appreciate them. They hold a very special place in my heart.

                                         Ron Kenoly
                                    Ambassador of Praise
                                  Jubilee Christian Center

Contents

Author's Introduction

My chest itched like crazy after the 24 hour journey to Jerusalem. I wished I hadn't come, that I could have stayed home in San Jose and nursed my shingles back to health.

"Are you okay?" whispered Carla from across our hotel bed. Petite with long blond hair, her concerned smile reassured me, but didn't stop the itching.

"No," I grumbled. "I'm grumpy from jet lag, and I can't sleep."

"Poor baby. Maybe this can be a vacation for you," my wife encouraged. "You've been working really hard at the church. Why don't you just let the camera crew take care of the documentary for Dr. Cho?"

I thought about the church we pastored back in San Jose. Our church had grown over 15 years from just Carla and me to six thousand members. Hispanics, African-Americans, Asians, and Caucasians worshipped side by side every week—a real sign of the Holy Spirit's blessing.

We had come to Jerusalem for a Church Growth International conference. Dr. David Yonggi Cho—who pastors a church in Seoul, Korea with 700,000 members—had organized the trip and appointed me head of the camera team. We were honoring the 2000th birthday of Christ, and the 3000th anniversary of King David's liberation of Jerusalem from the Jebusites.

There would be several days of teachings, group visits to historic sites, and a climactic March for Jesus. We had been given special permission to march from the Jerusalem Conference Center to the Knesset Parliament. Dr. Robert Schuller, one of the best known pastors in the world, would be joining us.

As I lay there scratching my shingles, little did I know that Dr. Cho would ask Carla and me to lead the March for Jesus. Nor could I foresee that Dr. Schuller would have to leave early, and that I would be invited to give the closing address.

It's just as well that God works in mysterious ways, because if I had known, the anxiety would have been too much. Yet the fact that I was placed in such a position of leadership is the story of every Christian. It is the great reversal in action—that God chooses the least among humans to become the greatest in His kingdom.

My spiritual autobiography is about that kingdom, the kingdom of God on earth and in heaven. Because as I opened my mouth to give the closing address in Jerusalem, I knew full well that in choosing me, God had chosen a hard-headed ironworker, former karate instructor to Hell's Angels, and the least likely candidate for the celebration of His Son's glory.

Have you found God yet? If not, maybe my story can help you, because for the longest time I didn't care if He existed.

PART ONE:

ENTERING THE KINGDOM

"The time is fulfilled,

and the kingdom of God is at hand.

Repent, and believe in the gospel."

—Mark 1:15

Dick Bernal

CHAPTER 1

"My Father Owns a Gas Station"

I grew up in Watsonville, a sleepy agricultural town in Northern California. My parents divorced before I was two years old, but I got plenty of love and security from my mother, two older sisters, and wonderful grandparents. Because my mother worked, my grandmother played a major role in shaping my young life.

My Uncle Dick drowned in 1941 while saving a woman's life in a flash flood. When I was born three years later, my mom named me after him, I think to help fill a void left by his death. Uncle Dick had been posthumously awarded the Wellman's medal of honor for sacrificing his life for another. As a boy I wore this bronze medal on a chain around my neck. Today the medal is a tender reminder of God's call on me to spend my life in the service of others. But I'm getting ahead of myself.

In spite of death and divorce in our extended family, ours was not a sad house. In fact, there was lots of laughter. Grandma had a kind of innocent humor that kept me in stitches. Once the Dodgers were playing the Giants on television. Sandy Koufax was ripping in the fast balls and striking out player after player. Grandma sat on the edge of the sofa, squinting at the TV. Finally, she said,

"That Sandy fellow isn't very nice. He's throwing the ball so fast that those poor boys can't hit it!"

My sisters, Judy and Juanita, became two of my closest friends. I'd be curious and wide eyed as they would drag me around town.

My first day of kindergarten was in September, 1949. I could hardly sleep the night before. *Oh boy*, I thought. *Now I can go along with my two big sisters to Freedom Elementary School!* My kindergarten teacher would be Miss Tyman, who had taught both Judy and Juanita.

The next morning Grandma took me by the hand and led me into what seemed a cavernous room. Thirty-three little desks were neatly lined up with name tags in place. Grandma carefully looked for Dickie Bernal's name.

"There it is Dickie!" she exclaimed, pointing to one near the back.

I sat down and my friend Gary Goldman plopped down next to me. We grinned at each other. Gary was a strange looking kid. He had a shock of white hair that stood straight up. No amount of butch wax would tame that mop. He was a forerunner to Rod Stewart, the English rock star who years later made a fashion statement with the same hairdo.

Miss Tyman began the day by suggesting that each of us stand, one by one, and tell our new classmates what our fathers did for a living. I felt panicky and found it hard to breathe. Daddy? My father was a stranger to me. He was a big dark-haired handsome fellow, but I had no idea what he did. Oh, he'd show up every few months with a toy or a new dollar for us kids. Then he'd make Mama cry. I didn't have a clue about how to relate to him.

One by one the kids stood up, ever so proud to announce their fathers' vocations. It was Gary's turn. Gary popped up, stuck out his chest, looked around the room and declared, "My father owns a gas station."

My turn came. Miss Tyman asked, "Dickie, what does your father do for a living?" I wanted to run home. Slowly—I mean slower than slow—I rose to my feet. I glanced at Grandma out of the corner of my eye. She gave me one of those looks only Grandma could give: "Honey boy, I love you but lie and you die!"

I looked back at Miss Tyman and took a deep breath. Squirming like a rabbit caught in a trap, I whispered, "My father owns a gas station too." Then I sat down as fast as humanly possible. It seemed like an eternity before I mustered the courage to look Grandma's way. Her expression was unmistakable: "I'll see you later, Sonny boy."

I'm dead meat, I thought.

Walking home that day I kicked every rock, cigarette butt, soda can—anything kickable. I walked into the house and was greeted with a command. "Go get me a switch, young man."

"Okay Grandma," I answered, trying to act brave. I had been through the ritual before. Grandma was small but had a swing on her like Babe Ruth. I gave her my hand-picked instrument of punishment. She turned it over in her hands, making sure it passed the spanking specs. It did. Telling me to bend over, she said, "Shame on you, Dickie! Never lie no matter what."

Old lady, I'd rather take a beating any day than feel shame again, I thought to myself. At four years and eleven months of age, I figured that lying was better than feeling embarrassed.

> *All we like sheep have gone astray;*
> *We have turned, every one, to his own way.*
> *—Isaiah 53:6*

Dick Bernal

CHAPTER 2

Who Is God?

During my grade school years in Watsonville, my friends were Japanese, Mexican, and Jewish. I didn't think that this was unusual until other kids made racial remarks that seemed mean to me. One of my Japanese friends taught me how to count to ten in Japanese. I remember feeling sorry for my Mexican friend Tommy whose bedroom had cracks clear through it, but envied him for his warm and loving Dad and Mom.

I loved Saturday afternoon matinees, especially the adventure movies set in mysterious places like India or Africa. Movies like *Gunga Din* and *Sabu*, the jungle boy. Cobras and tigers fascinated me.

But the biggest thing that happened in those years was television! "Can you believe it?" I asked Tommy when we saw the black and white picture on the screen for the first time. "It's like having your own movie theater at home!"

A rich kid in our neighborhood lived in a two-story house. His parents had a gardener, a new station wagon with wood-like paneling, and best of all, a television set. I never really liked that boy until his dad bought the television. Then he quickly became the most popular boy on our block. We spent a lot of time at his house, especially after school when *Howdy Doody* came on.

Uncle Bob, Milton Berle, Ed Sullivan, and of course, the Lone Ranger, all became weekly friends. Before long we owned a television of our own. No longer did I play kick-the-can or hide-and-go-seek until dark. In retrospect, I believe it was healthier playing our favorite games. But at the time we called it progress.

There were not a lot of programs on Saturday afternoons that we watched, except for a very different kind of telecast that came on about 4:00 p.m. The telecast was from an enormous tent packed with thousands of people, and featured a preacher from Tulsa named Oral Roberts. This man preached like a house on fire about the wages of sin, and how only God's grace and mercy could save people from eternal damnation.

Then he would do something most odd. He would sit on a chair, lay his hand on the head of each person in a long line, and yell, "Be healed!"

When he did this his head would jerk and his hair would fly around. Sweat poured down his face. Even to many people who were faithful churchgoers, his program was a real wild scene. All of us were captivated by the entire scenario. Once in awhile, one of the grown-ups in the room would remark, "Do you suppose this is all real?" None of us dared say it was a fake for fear of God's wrath, so we just sat there wondering in silence. Not being church-going folks, we had no idea what was real and what was not.

The whole God-and-Jesus thing became a little confusing for me. Often Grandma read her Bible late at night. She obviously revered the Word of God, although she never commented on it. But she sure believed in honesty, clean living, and the respect of children for their elders.

Grandma really enjoyed a religious program by Bishop Fulton Sheen. I would watch this oddly dressed man with the piercing eyes and reassuring voice. He spoke of God's goodness and love.

One Saturday afternoon, a couple of us guys sneaked into a big Roman Catholic church on Main Street to check things out. After daring and double-dog daring one another, we tiptoed through the door and took a look. The big gothic edifice sent chills up my spine. It reminded me of a movie I once saw about a deformed man, *The Hunchback of Notre Dame.* To make things even spookier, there was a school next door named Notre Dame.

We inched ourselves down the aisle. There were candles lit up toward the front of the church. The flickering glow charged the atmosphere with mystery. We made it down to a rail, where I stared up at a poor, tormented individual hanging on a huge cross. His eyes were looking upward as if he were crying out for help from some invisible force. His face, hands, and feet had blood on them. We had begun inching backwards toward the door, when suddenly the sound of footsteps from behind a side curtain startled me.

"Run for it!" I yelled.

We hit the front door running and didn't stop until we passed the graveyard on Freedom Boulevard. Then we all laughed like crazy, figuring we had tempted fate and gotten out alive. Oddly enough, we never talked about that day again. Yet the images I had encountered—especially the man on the cross—remained with me a long time. I remember lying on my bed thinking how lonely the man looked.

Why did they hang him on a cross? I asked myself. *What did he do to deserve such a horrible death?*

At the other end of the religious spectrum was the little storefront Pentecostal Holiness church down near the Pajaro River, next door to the Center Theater. When my ten-year-old buddies and I stood in line for the Sunday morning matinee, we'd hear the folks inside the little church shouting, whooping, and hollering. It seemed you could hear them for a mile. When we came out of the movie theater, they'd still be at it. What in the world was going on in there?

One Sunday afternoon, we decided to sneak in and see for ourselves. We slipped through the front door, trying to be incon-spicuous. Forty to fifty adults were jumping up and down, hands raised as if someone had a gun to their backs. Their eyes looked dazed and they were yelling all kinds of things. Some were speaking a strange foreign language I had never heard before. One big black lady was rolling around on the floor as if she was having a seizure or something. Without a word, we beat it for the door at the same time. We were scared that we'd catch whatever was wrong with them.

Every now and then a thought would pester me. *Who is God anyway?* Did God live on a cross in that scary church down on Main, or did He hang out with the weird people next to the theater? Or was God with Oral Roberts in that big tent? What about Bishop Sheen in his strange costume? Did he speak for God?

That Christmas I played the role of an extra shepherd in the school Nativity play. As I gazed down at the little doll in the manger, I wondered who Jesus was. *Jesus must be a good guy, because He gets me out of school for two weeks at Christmas and another week at Easter.* But why would such a nice man have to die such a terrible death?

Finally, I decided that you must understand all this after you grow up. My folks surely never discussed it.

MY FIRST PRAYER

The next fall I felt big and important going into the sixth grade. Along with my buddy David, I was asked to try out for the school's basketball team. Each year an outstanding sixth grader was asked to join the seventh and eighth graders' A or B squad. Hey, this was big time! You would get to travel all the way to Salinas or even up to Hollister. Also, you could wear the blue and white colors of Freedom Elementary Union in front of cheering masses. Was there anything in the whole world more important than my making the team? No way!

My only obstacle was David. He was a good free-throw shooter, but I had a better jump shot from the floor. Plus, I was an inch taller and had all the right moves. No problem!

The night before the team members were chosen, I figured

a little prayer wouldn't hurt. Maybe it would give me the extra edge. I had never prayed before, because I had never wanted anything this badly. I lay in bed that night staring at the ceiling, trying my best to picture this God no one had ever really told me about. I came up with a thin and serious looking Santa Claus.

Yep, that is probably pretty much the way he looks, I thought as I began to pray. "Dear God, please let me be the one picked for our basketball team. I'll be a good boy. I'll help Mom and Grandma around the house more. Really, I will, and well, it means a whole lot to me... Amen."

Of course, I did not tell God how impressed the girls at school would be if I made the team, especially Maureen. I had heard she kind of liked me—a little bit, anyway. Bolstered by my first conversation with God Almighty, I confidently dozed off, dreaming of shooting swishers that would triumphantly win games in the last three seconds. Glory would be mine as a superstar.

The next day I stood in front of the coach's office and read the ten names of the new team. The tenth name was David Betz, not Dick Bernal. My life crumbled before me. How could God do this to me? I decided God was either cruel or a poor judge of basketball talent. As everyone congratulated my pal David, I slunk down the hallway holding back tears of disappointment.

I decided later that day that if I was going to accomplish great things in life, it would have to be on my own. I couldn't trust God or anyone else for help. I would make my own dreams come true!

There is a way that seems right to a man,
But its end is the way of death.
—Proverbs 16:25

Dick Bernal

CHAPTER 3

What Makes Life Worth Living?

In 1957 we moved from sleepy little Watsonville to San Jose. I was coming of age as a teenager. The new fin-tailed car that Chevrolet put out was the talk of the town. That year Elvis belted out "You Ain't Nothin' But a Hound Dog," his hips shimmying on the Ed Sullivan show.

As a lowly high school freshman, I wore my freshman's beanie cap to the football games and cheered louder than anyone else. I really wanted to feel accepted, but found myself the brunt of senior jokes and snickers instead.

The upperclassmen drove hot cars, shaved, and flexed their biceps at the girls. I'd pull up to school on my red bicycle, fighting pimples and sporting a chin covered with peach fuzz. My 126 pounds barely covered my six-foot frame.

In an effort to look cool, I'd don a rugged pair of blue jeans pegged just right, slip on a white T-shirt, and turn up the collar of my denim jacket. Add to that a little Clearasil, a waterfall hairdo, and a splash of cologne and maybe I could turn a girl's head, too.

It wasn't too long before I realized that my bike had to go. One day I gave it to a younger kid and started hoofing it to school.

About that time, my mother remarried. Her new husband was a nice man named Emmett, whose first wife was deceased. He had been left with four children, so all of us moved into the same house.

My oldest stepbrother, Fritz, had an old Ford pickup which begged me to hot-wire it. One night around midnight, my friend Les and I fired it up and took off for a spin. Les figured I knew how to drive, and I was sure he was a seasoned pro. We barreled along for two whole miles before the engine blew up. In a downpour of rain, we pushed the truck all the way back.

The sun peaked over the horizon as we inched the dead truck back up the sloping driveway, leaving it exactly where it had been parked before. Mom couldn't understand why Les and I slept in until noon. Poor old Fritz tinkered around out there for hours trying to figure out what had happened to his pride and joy.

I finally got up and made my way outside. Innocently, I strolled around the truck. Fritz stood there scratching his chin, but Emmett shot me a knowing glance that nearly stopped my heart. *My stepfather knew!*

Emmett really won me over when he winked to me, and then said to Fritz, "Well, son, I guess she just up and died."

THE SHIRT OFF MY BACK

The summer of 1960 was hot and long. I was too young to get a work permit. All my friends over sixteen were working at the local cannery making good money, enough to buy themselves cars. On Saturdays, they'd drive to school, wash and wax the love of their life, and plan the strategy for cruising around town that night. I tagged along riding shotgun, waving at the girls, and dreaming of the day when I could proudly weave through the drive-ins in my own car. Life was not fair.

Les dropped in one afternoon in July. "Ever hear of hops, Dickie?" he asked excitedly.

"Hops? What's hops?"

"My dad has arranged for you and me to work picking hops on his friend's ranch up near Sacramento for the rest of the summer!" he exclaimed. "They use hops for making beer. And if we work six days a week, ten hours a day, guess what?"

"We'll make enough money to buy a car?" I blurted out.

"Yup. More than $300 a month. I figured it out on paper."

Wow! We could both have cars by the time our junior year started. Now that made life worth living. Les and I were going to be sixteen and popular!

Mom and Grandma reluctantly agreed to let me go up to the hops ranch with Les. As we turned into the ranch's long, dusty driveway, the smell of freshly cut alfalfa hung thick in the afternoon air. "Lazy J Ranch" was painted on one of the large silos in the distance. The hops fields stretched out before us like an endless ocean of green.

When we walked into the employment trailer, a burly man named Sam stood up. He wore a faded flannel shirt rolled up past his bulging biceps. I could see an anchor tattooed on the back of his left hand. He had a couple of cigarettes tucked into his front shirt pocket. His weather-beaten cowboy hat looked cool.

"Hello boys," he said, extending a big hand. "You must be Les and Dick. Here are some papers to sign so we can get goin'."

Les' Dad had called ahead and made arrangements for us. We found out later that these arrangements included instructions to Sam to work us into the ground, and not let us get away with anything.

Sam drove us out to the fields and showed us where we would be loading hops onto the back of trucks. He said that the workday started with breakfast at 5:30 a.m. We'd be out in the fields by 6:30, get a thirty-minute break for lunch, and work until 5 p.m. Sam told us we had to wear gloves because of something called "hop poisoning," but I didn't dare ask him what that meant.

Bernal, how bad do you want a car? I asked myself. *The only way you're going to get one is to work your butt off.*

Sam drove us back over to the crew quarters. The interior

looked like an army barracks with twenty cots lined up on each side. Sam picked us out two cots by the door. He pointed to the makeshift closet for our clothes. The toilets and showers looked pretty cramped.

"Supper's at 7:00 in the mess hall, boys," he said, leaving Les and me sitting on our bunks. The screen door creaked open and a group of men entered the barracks. Dusty and tired from their day in the hops fields, I noticed that they were either black or Mexican—no Caucasians in the bunch. All were in their thirties or forties.

One by one they eyed us up and down. One said, "My, my, what have we here? What are your names, boys?"

I jumped up quickly and answered, "My name is Dickie, and this is my friend Les."

One six-foot-seven African-American said his name was Joe Brown. "Where you from?" Joe asked.

"San Jose," I said.

He laughed. "Well, I don't like the name 'Dickie', so I'm going to call you 'San Jose Slim.'" I found out later that Joe Brown wasn't just creative with nicknames. He could also quote Edgar Allan Poe and cite some Scripture.

I swallowed hard. "That's fine, sir. You can call me anything you want."

Just then the rest of the men came in. They looked real tough. I felt my stomach clench up. We found out later that all these guys were convicts out on work furlough to help support their families.

That night in the mess hall, Les whispered to me, "Can you believe this? Can you believe we're going to be living with these guys all summer long? Think we'll get hurt?"

A sense of optimism welled up inside me. I shrugged my shoulders. "Naw, we'll be all right. They seem to be a nice sort."

Les looked at me with disbelieving eyes. "Oh yeah?"

After dinner, we walked back to the barracks. Feeling a little timid, we walked up and down the aisle watching the men playing cards and shaking dice. One man strummed a guitar and another guy blew his harmonica. A few dozed in their bunks. Others simply stared up at the ceiling, deep in thought. We caught a few smiles as we walked around. I felt that they were taking to us. At least I hoped so.

The next day, the work supervisor put Les on one truck and me on another. When we came back in for lunch, I saw Les standing over by the office. I walked over and asked, "What are you doing?"

"I got fired this morning," he said. "I'm going back home. My folks are on the way to pick me up. Let's get out of this place!"

"Fired! How did you get fired?"

"Some guy said something to me that I didn't like." Les shook his head. "I talked back to him, and they fired me. So I'm going home. Are you ready to go?"

I thought about it, then said, "No, I'm not going anywhere. I came up here to work, and I want to make enough money for a car. Besides, I'm not a quitter."

Les shrugged. "Have it your way."

Later that afternoon, Les' parents arrived. In a flash he was gone. Now I was going this alone—with 29 black guys and one Mexican American.

The men in the barracks chorused, "Hey, San Jose, what happened to your friend?"

"He got fired," I said. They all whooped with laughter.

"Well, boy," one man named Hammer chuckled, "you probably won't make it much longer yourself. This ain't work fit for a boy."

You just watch me, I thought. *I can hang in there with the toughest.*

That night, I went for a walk. Out under the stars I took a deep breath and gazed up at the heavens. "I will make it," I said out loud. "I will win."

On Sundays the men all went into town. That left me by myself in the barracks with nothing to do. I asked Sam if there was some way I could make a little extra money.

"Sure," he said. "You can scrub out the hoppers on Sunday. It's pretty hard work, but I'll pay you a little extra."

I took the job and started working ten hours on Sundays and a couple of hours overtime each night. It was grimy, back-breaking work, but the 1954 Oldsmobile of my dreams kept me going. That baby was going to cost me $400.

In the little spare time that I had, I learned how to box from a thin jive-talkin' guy named Calhoun. Calhoun was cool, streetwise, and about 24. He carefully combed his curly black hair, even though his clothes and shoes were tattered. When he'd talk about the past in New York City, his eyes would glaze over with the rough life he'd had. Calhoun always wanted to beat me at running or boxing, but he wasn't mean about it. I grew quite attached to Calhoun.

At summer's end the hops season came to a close. The long hard days were finally over. I knew I was going to miss these guys. Joe Brown had become a kind of guardian angel. The guys who played guitar and harmonica had taught me several songs. Calhoun was like an older brother.

On the day I was to leave, my stepfather came to pick me up, and boy, did his eyes get big when he saw my ethnic work mates. I hugged each one of them, saving Calhoun for last. There were some wet eyes. Mine among them.

An impulse came over me and I handed my duffel bag to Calhoun. In it were my leather work gloves, Red Wing workboots and work socks, my work shirt and jeans. I knew we were about the same size. Calhoun started crying and hugged me tightly. Brushing away a tear, I took off my white hard-hat, and placed it on his head. He smiled broadly.

I felt a tug on my heart that I'll never forget when I turned away and got in the car. I kept wondering what would become of my new-found friends. I felt a rush of frustration and empathy for all blacks and Mexicans, as if I was one of them suffering the pangs of bigotry and persecution. This experience awakened my first stirrings of compassion for people.

And I had learned something about myself—that I could hang in there when things got tough. I would return to my junior year in high school as more of a veteran of life.

But this wasn't to last. The tender roots of self-dignity and caring for others were not deep enough to withstand the self-willed tempest of my roaring twenties.

> *Am I my brother's keeper?*
> *—Genesis 4:9*

Dick Bernal

CHAPTER 4

Roaring Twenties

My high school graduation in 1962 coincided with a period of transition in America. If I had a time in my life that I could do over, it would be the years from 1962 to 1974. President John F. Kennedy was assassinated. America lost her innocence. And so did I. Then came Vietnam, the hippie movement, Watergate, the assassination of Martin Luther King, and the Charles Manson murders. Things got freaky.

The days of *Leave It to Beaver, Father Knows Best, and Mr. Ed* were long gone. The innocent themes of the music popular during my high school years were replaced by lyrics about rebellion and cynicism.

A friend got me a good job as an ironworker, making union wages. Monday through Friday I was a good ol' boy. But come Friday night, I would grab my bellbottoms, headband, and beads, and make the scene in San Francisco. My buddies and I hung out at Bill Graham's Filmore West. Jimmy Hendrix. Janis Joplin. Grace Slick. Iron Butterfly. Country Joe and the Fish. Blue Cheer. We saw them all. I'd drop acid or swallow some magic mushrooms to soar with the music.

My favorite was mescaline in spite of the bitter pungent taste. This drug created a rushing sensation. Everywhere I looked colors became bright and vivid, probably because my pupils were so dilated. The mescaline made everything seem hysterically funny. The next morning my cheek muscles would be sore from laughing so hard. We'd take our reds to get off our whites and go listen to the blues. Some of these weekends turned into a blurred psychedelic haze.

Even though I was wreaking havoc on my body every weekend, I was taking karate to stay in shape. I studied at a Korean style dojo on Alameda Street in old San Jose. I earned a brown belt and became assistant instructor on Monday and Wednesday nights.

HELL'S ANGELS

A bunch of Hell's Angels piled into the karate dojo one night. They told my instructor that they wanted to improve their street-fighting skills. The instructor assigned me the job of taking them through calisthenics and loosening them up with basic kicks and punches.

After a few weeks, I started making friends with these guys. I was attracted by their loyalty and camaraderie, as misguided as it was. I was impressed that they would take a bullet for each other, and never rat out on their buddies if one was interrogated by the police. Oddly, the Hell's Angels provided my first example of a covenant in action—a kind of "nothing can come between us" fraternity.

I was lured closer to their lifestyle by the excitement that swirled around them. As a kid I had read Zane Grey and Louis L'Amour. These Hell's Angels seemed like a throwback to those wild west days. They had their own rules and code of honor, spurning social norms. Yet there was an openness and transparency among them—a real bond of trust.

I drank and smoked dope at their parties, but got turned off when I'd see some of them jamming heroin needles into their arms. I remember one party in particular at a flophouse in Mountain View. The garage was filled with motorcycle parts. There wasn't any furniture to speak of because the house was used for parties.

About 100 people dropped by that night. Super loud music rocked the house. A new keg of beer was rolled into the living room every few minutes. One guy rode his Harley-Davidson into the living room and did a wheelie, before roaring out the back door.

One of the leaders named Billy liked me, even though I was somewhat of an outsider. I found myself staring at his girl-friend, who was a real knockout. A guy could get killed for doing something that stupid. Billy noticed me leering at her. But instead of getting mad, he walked over and offered her to me.

At that very moment I had taken a drag off an opium pipe. Within seconds I felt frozen against the wall. It took my total concentration to keep from falling on my face. Billy's girlfriend came over to ask if I was ready for her. I just gave her a glassy-eyed stare. I stood glued to the wall from one until five in the morning. I never tried opium again.

It wasn't long before I came to a crossroads with these guys. My Hell's Angels group came in for a karate lesson livid with rage. One of their bikes had been stolen. They had reconnoitered the area and found the bike. Leaving it there, they planned to go back and set a trap for the thieves.

"Hey Dick, you wanna have some fun tonight?"

"Sure," I said.

So there I was in a '52 Chevy torpedo-back, 50 yards from where the bike was hidden. We were crouched down low in the car. *This is really cool,* I thought. Just then I heard clicking sounds in the front and back seats. They were shoving magazines into pistols and talking about how they were going to kill the enemy very slowly.

My Grandma's voice went off in my head and I pictured her no-nonsense gaze: "Dicky, you shouldn't be here. Now you get out of this mess before you end up in jail!"

I said to the Man upstairs, if He existed, "Oh, get me outta this!" But I was too afraid to leave. I gabbed my way through the night, pretending everything was fine. Miraculously, nobody showed up. When the sun came up and I was able to leave the car, I vowed to ease out of my gang involvement over the next month. Since that time about five of the guys I knew have died, including Billy.

JESUS FREAKS

After a couple of years, all the deafening rock concerts started sounding alike to me. One night, a friend and I were listening to a band in San Francisco, when a young man followed me into the restroom. He wanted to sell me some hits of methadone. He was about nineteen, pleasant looking, but his brain was fried. I could barely make out his words as he stuttered and struggled to communicate. As one rock song of the day said, "He had tombstones in his eyes."

Bernal, I said to myself, *it's time to find a new way of living before you end up like this poor soul.*

During this time, the Jesus movement had broken out. Hundreds of zealots flooded the streets passing out tracts and witnessing. A group of former addicts approached me one night in front of the fairgrounds. Bless their hearts, they could see I was hell-bound, but boy, did they scare me! They were wild-eyed, shouting the name of Jesus, and wanting to cast devils out of me.

"Join us, brother. Leave the world of sin behind. Come be like us. Free! Jesus loves you, brother!"

"Uh, hey, I'm happy for you guys, really. It's great that you fellows have found religion. I would love to talk more, but I have to go. I have a really important appointment."

I needed to do some more research in living by my own rules and passions.

> *Since they didn't bother to acknowledge God,*
> *God quit bothering them and let them run loose.*
> *And then all hell broke loose.*
> *—Romans 1:28-29 THE MESSAGE*

CHAPTER 5

Like Father, Like Son

One evening I visited Dad at his house. He downed a few double shots of whiskey, then started lecturing me about how to fight. "Never kick a man in a fight," he declared.

"Why?" I asked. "A fight is a fight."

"If you're going to hit someone, hit him with your fist like a man. If I ever hear of you using your feet, I'll come after you and whip you myself."

Surprising myself, I fired back, "Oh, yeah? And who is going to help you?"

I had never talked back to Dad before. He looked stunned. We stared at each other like the gunfighters in *High Noon*. Casually, he tossed down another two fingers of whiskey and stood up. I tossed back my shot and stood up.

Dad's girlfriend came running out of the kitchen and tried to calm us down, but it was too late.

"So you think you're pretty quick, huh?" he challenged. "Then show me your stuff, boy." He got into a Jack Dempsey stance.

Great, this is just great, I said to myself. *What now, big*

*mouth. If I sit down, he'll think I'm a sissy. If I accept his chal-
lenge, someone might get hurt. Boy! I forgot how big Daddy is.*

"Dad, let me demonstrate what I've learned in karate. I am
going to kick you lightly under your left armpit. It'll be so fast you
can't block it, so just relax and don't move. Okay?"

My somewhat amused father replied, "Really? When are
you going to do all this?"

"Now," I yelled. I spun around with a wheel-kick. But I'd
had just enough liquor to throw off my timing. The powerful kick
struck my dad squarely in the side, breaking three of his ribs. He
wheezed and dropped like a sack of potatoes.

Dad lay there grasping his side for a moment, and then broke
into a pained laugh. "Boy, you're quick as lightning," he croaked.
"You think you could teach me that kick some day?"

A flood of mixed emotions hit me! I felt like dirt for deck-
ing my Dad, yet I was proud for gaining his respect.

RIDE'M COWBOY

Later, I tried a different tack for getting closer to my father.
Dad had been involved with horses and rodeos all his life. Yep, I
got a pair of cowboy boots, some Wranglers, a sharp-looking
Stetson, a buckstitch belt, and tried myself out on the rodeo circuit.

I signed up at a local rodeo and rode a big Brahma bull. To
my utter astonishment, I hung on to the ornery thing for the full
eight seconds! I liked the applause, too. So I figured I would get
real good at rodeoing, then invite the old man out to see me per-
form. Dad had always wanted me to be a cowboy like him, and I
needed his acceptance really bad. I felt obsessed with the notion of
becoming my dad's friend.

After a few months of jackpot bull riding, I had visions of
going professional and making a living out of it. Now seemed the
time to drop in on Dad. One Saturday, I stopped by his place to see
how he was doing.

When he opened the front door his jaw dropped. He looked
me over from top to bottom. "What ya been up to, cowboy?" he

asked, grinning like a possum. He seemed pleased with my new choice of attire.

"Oh, just a little rodeoing," I said. "I like bull riding best."

"Really?" Dad sounded surprised. "I'd like to come take a look sometime."

My heart quickened. I finally had his attention. "Well, next Friday I'll be riding out at the Rocking R Ranch," I said, trying to cover my excitement.

"I know the place," he said. "I'll be there."

I could hardly believe it. In all the years that I had played sports in grammar and high school, Dad never once came to watch or cheer me on. When teammates would ask where he was, I'd say he was too busy working, knowing all the while that he was drunk or out womanizing.

Friday night came and I bolstered my confidence with a half pint of blended whiskey. I scanned the stands for my dad. There he was, all decked out in western finery, sitting with his girlfriend Julie.

My first draw was a young bull called Booger Red. He had a bad reputation for scraping off riders along the fence. I eased down on the bull and wrapped the bucking rope around my left hand, thinking, *How am I going to keep Red from heading for the fence?*

"Ready, Dick?" shouted the handler.

"Outside!" I yelled, having taken that phrase from a real cowboy.

I do not know to this day what got into that crazy bull, but he jumped like a frog and landed on all fours, jarring every bone in my body. Then he did a 180-degree turn and jumped right back into the chute. I sailed right off him when he stopped, landing head first in six inches of wet manure.

Above the laughter of the crowd, I could hear my dad howling with glee, slapping his leg as if he had just seen the funniest thing in his life. "Ride'm, cowboy," he yelled. I sat up and did the only thing I could. I laughed too.

I decided the cowboy life was not for me. But more than

that, I learned that I was barking up the wrong tree in striving to get my earthly father's approval.

The LORD is longsuffering and abundant in mercy, forgiving iniquity
and transgression; but He by no means clears the guilty,
visiting the iniquity of the fathers on the children
to the third and fourth generation.
—Numbers 14:18

CHAPTER 6

Taste of Mortality

In my late twenties I moved in with another bachelor named Jerry. He had just gone through a divorce and welcomed my company. I was trying to offset my lonely feelings. Before long Jerry's place was buzzing with booze, pot, and loud music. If life was a cruel joke, at least we could make up our own punch lines.

Foot loose and fancy free, I had quit pursuing and even speaking to my dad. The swinging bachelor's life was for me. No nagging wife making me come home right after work. No kids dragging me down to the ball park. Just me to make happy.

I liked coming and going as I pleased and spending all my money on myself. I went out with a different girl whenever I wanted. I was the envy of all the guys at work. If there was a heaven on earth, this was surely it.

Yeah? Then why did I feel so miserable? Deep down inside, I had to admit that I really did want someone to come home to every night. I wanted to care and be cared for. I needed love.

My attempt at marriage at nineteen had been an absolute flop. The word commitment was not in my vocabulary. To me, the bond between a man and a woman was a physical thing that lasted for a short while until things got boring. I had no idea about the work and effort that makes for a successful marriage. Out of the failure of my first marriage, for which I take full blame, came a beautiful child who today has grown into a fine young man.

When Adam was a young boy, I felt uneasy around him. I felt guilty for doing the same thing to him that my dad had done to me. But I had no power to break the curse over my life. The sins of the father had been passed down once again. I figured I had made my own bed, so I had to accept my fate.

Bernal, I thought, *you're incapable of a normal family life, just like your dad. You will undoubtedly die young, so live hard and fast, and get it all before it gets you.*

HEAVEN AND HELL

I hadn't spoken to Dad in eight months. When I'd gone back to wearing my hippie outfit with long hair and bell bottoms, he had blown his stack. "Don't ever come to visit me looking like that!" he had yelled. So I didn't. Our yelling match left us both too proud to make amends.

I was shocked beyond belief when Dad died of a heart attack in December of 1970. He was only in his mid-fifties, but the wear and tear of his rough lifestyle got the best of him. One minute he was in the world, a phone call away, and the next minute he was gone forever.

The finality of his death really hit me when I saw Dad laying in the coffin at his funeral three days later. I felt cheated that he'd died before I'd got a chance to remedy our rift. *Where is Dad now?* I wondered. I surely hoped he was in heaven and not in hell.

At the funeral, my step-brother Chris looked dreadful. He couldn't believe our dad had died. That week he became deeply depressed, even suicidal. I think the first pastoring I ever did was putting my arm around Chris' shoulder and comforting him. But I didn't have any real tools for helping people. So I bought him a six-pack to ease his despair. Still, I cared more about helping him through his dark valley than attending to my own pain.

Our family doctor had pointed out that heart disease ran in the male members of my family. Most had died young. My dad's first heart attack had been 12 years earlier.

The doctor had picked up the pattern of high blood pressure and a fluttering heart when I was 19. My smoking and drug and alcohol abuse didn't help my occasional dizziness and heart palpitations.

CLOSE CALL

One night in early 1974 I was awakened out of a very deep sleep. Adrenalin rushed through me, and a sense of alarm gripped me. I lay there with eyes open, feeling a strange sensation passing through my toes and feet. This electric tingling began to creep up my legs until it reached my lower back, and then it stopped momentarily. My whole lower body felt numb and lifeless. Slowly the sensation began to crawl almost animal-like up my spine. *What in the world was happening to me? Dear God, I'm not dreaming. This is real!*

Eventually, the sensation reached the base of my neck. An explosion of crimson flashed across my vision. There was no pain. Then brilliant red turned to black. The next thing I knew I was hovering like a hummingbird over my body, looking down at what had been Dick Bernal.

How sad he looks, I thought.

I was hovering about 18 inches below the ceiling of my bedroom, totally aware of my surroundings, and looking down on the body that housed Dick Bernal. I thought to myself, *Bernal, your body is dead, but you are still alive. Now what?* I wondered. *Where am I going? Will someone come for me?*

I felt free, yet perplexed, not knowing what the next moment would hold. As I pondered my predicament, I began to sink. I felt pulled back down into my body by a strange force. I reentered my body right through the chest area. The next thing I knew, I was lying flat on my back in bed staring up at the ceiling.

Life began to flow back into my body. In an exact reversal of the previous process, the tingling sensation at the base of my neck progressed down my spine and into my legs.

I jumped out of bed, turned on all the lights, and flipped on the television. I sat down and nervously lit a cigarette. For three hours I sat deep in thought, smoking and shaking my head in disbelief. Finally, the rays of the early morning sun broke over the Mount Hamilton range. I got dressed and ready for work.

I drove to Stanford University where I was overseeing a hospital remodeling project. I was convinced that I had had a stroke and died, but for some unexplainable reason I was still alive.

Years later, I told Carla about the whole experience. "Honey," she said, "the hand of the Lord on you spared your life. He knew that you would accept His call to the ministry."

My heart is severely pained within me,
And the terrors of death have fallen upon me.
—Psalms 55:4

CHAPTER 7

Something More

Life seemed bleak at 30. I was still living like a nomad, everything I owned fitting into the trunk of my car. I felt out of touch with my twelve-year-old son, who was being reared by another man. My friends were all alcoholics or addicts. On top of that, my job as an iron worker was for very young men. I had maybe another ten years before my back would give out.

I felt that if I went to one more party, I was headed for a jump off the Golden Gate Bridge. My favorite whiskey now tasted like battery acid. The girls in the clubs all looked and sounded alike. Like soulless mannequins, they'd whisper to every lonely Joe: "Hey, what's your name? I'll bet you are a Leo. Wanna have some fun?" Egads! Wasn't there anything more to life?

The day after a lackluster Christmas in 1974, my roommate and I were at our local watering hole drinking long-neck Budweisers, playing pool, and listening to Merle, Waylon, and Willie sing about their problems.

"I'm sick of this place, Jerry," I said, feeling the post-holiday blues. "Let's go somewhere else. I need a change of scenery tonight."

There was a nicer place right up the road where a different crowd hung out. We pulled into the parking lot, and I wondered why there were only one or two cars.

"Is it closed?" I asked.

"Well, we'll soon find out," said Jerry. He jumped out and tried the front door.

"They're open," he called as he motioned me to follow him. When we walked in, the bartender looked pleased that someone had showed up.

"What brings you boys out tonight?" he asked cheerfully.

"Just looking for a little after-Christmas action," said Jerry.

"Boy, you two sure picked the wrong night. Everyone is at home resting up for New Year's Eve."

Just then the door opened. In walked two very attractive girls. Jerry and I grinned at the bartender, who winked back. Jerry elbowed me to go into action with my smooth operator routine, which I'd done dozens of times before. No big deal. I'd walk up to a ladies' table, introduce myself, and ask one of them to dance.

I headed straight for the red-head facing me. "Hi. Would you like to dance with me?"

"No, thanks," she said. "I'm married."

"Oh, too bad. How about you?" I asked the other one whose back had been turned to me.

"No, thanks," she said, still with her back to me and staring at the other girl.

I liked her long blonde hair and persisted. "Come on, let's dance." My insides yelled at me that she wasn't interested and to beat it. But somehow I wouldn't budge. I had seen other guys pester pretty girls and had gotten in more than one fight coming to their rescue. Here I was doing exactly what I hated, but for some strange reason, I could not leave that table. What was wrong with me?

"Please, just one dance—pretty please?"

As I bent over the table, the gold cross I wore around my

neck fell out of my unbuttoned shirt. I felt that if a cross was good enough for Elvis and Tom Jones to wear, why not me?

The blonde woman stared at the cross and said, "Okay. Just one."

As she stood up, I noticed how pretty she was—a real angel to me. The band was playing short versions of old standards, probably because of the empty dance floor. The music stopped much too quickly. Just my luck!

"What's your name?" I asked hurriedly as she sat down.

"Carla, and this is my sister, Karen. We haven't seen each other for a long time, so we're catching up on family news. Thank you. Good-bye."

"Hey, why don't I join you, and you can talk all you want?"

The whole time I was saying to myself, *Bernal, don't be a jerk. Leave these two sweet sisters alone. You're bugging them. It's obvious they have other things on their minds.*

But no, I pulled up a chair and sat down next to them. I smiled as they went on and on about family events. When I'd put in my two-cents they'd offer polite smiles and continue talking to each other. As the evening wore on, it was getting time for working people to go home. I asked Carla if she wanted to have dinner with me the next night. She stared at me without saying anything. But when I suggested Chinese food, she said that Chinese was her favorite.

"Great," I said. "Give me your address and phone number. I'll call right before I drop by."

Carla told me later that she said to Karen on their way home, "Why did I say yes? I'm not looking for anyone, nor do I want to go out with him tomorrow night."

The next night I found myself sharing with this beautiful stranger my dream of a normal life—marriage, children, a house with a picket fence, a vegetable garden, dogs and cats, the whole bit. I shared my past failures and my fears of an uncertain future. I unashamedly bared my heart and soul.

For some reason, it was so easy to talk to her. There was something different about this woman that I couldn't put my finger on. I had prided myself on my knowledge of women. Being around more women than men most of my life, I felt I pretty much understood their ways, moods, and mannerisms. But I had never encountered this kind of girl before. It was not just her looks, because I had dated very good-looking girls. It was deeper than that. She had this warm inner glow. Her sister had it too. I wondered what it was.

The following Saturday, I had extra tickets to a concert in Berkeley, so I asked Carla if she and her sister wanted to go. The two girls piled into my coupe and we headed for the concert. Actually, I had a date with another girl who was waiting for me in front of the theater. As awkward as all this was, I had not wanted to miss a chance to be with Carla. Everyone made the best of the situation and we all walked in together.

As the days and weeks passed, Carla and I became virtually inseparable. One day, some of her relatives arrived from Oklahoma. Carla invited me to a barbecue at her mother's house in Hayward. She had neglected to tell me, however, that these were all church-going people. In I waltzed with my customary case of beer, a gallon of cheap wine, and a trusty cigarette dangling out of the corner of my mouth. In my circle of friends, you never showed up for a party empty-handed.

I never saw so much iced tea and so many soft drinks in all my life! I was the only one smoking and drinking. Still, I had a great time talking sports, construction work, and fishing with the visiting male relatives. They seemed to enjoy my company, and I felt completely at home. Carla seemed proud as punch showing off her new beau.

As Carla and I were getting ready to leave, her mother followed us out to the car and said, "Daddy and I are surely praying for you kids."

Driving Carla home to her sister's, I could not shake those words out of my mind—"We are praying for you." No one had ever told me, "I am praying for you." Someone was talking to God about me. How about that!

The next Saturday Carla was cutting my hair. "Honey," I

said, "tell me about the Bible and church. What is a Baptist anyway?"

She began to share a little about Jesus. Then she dropped a Bible in my lap. I handled it cautiously at first, then began to leaf through it as if I knew exactly what I was doing.

I thought to myself, *How do you pronounce Deuteronomy? For goodness sakes, how can anyone understand this stuff.* I flipped to another book of the Old Testament. *Numbers. Hmmm. Man, how does this relate to anything? This is 1975. I guess some people get something out of this, but I'm not one of them.*

"What do you think?" Carla asked excitedly.

"I will have to really get into this later," I lied. *Much later,* I thought to myself.

Our love grew deeper over that year. My son Adam approved wholeheartedly of Carla, and she fell in love with him. On November 29, 1975, we exchanged our vows in front of the Rev. Johnny B. Love, who married us in Lake Tahoe, Nevada.

A couple of friends joined us for the celebration. As the minister was reading the vows, I could tell Carla was listening intently to the Bible passages. I just wanted to finish the "I do" part and get on with the party.

My little wife looked so beautiful and radiant. I was fighting the flu, but still had a great time.

Gone were my carefree bachelor days, and I had no regrets. Carla was a stabilizing factor in my life. The following morning a foot of new snow had fallen in the Tahoe Basin. The sun broke through by 9 a.m. What a splendid sight. Who knows? Maybe this beautiful day was a sign of things to come—a fresh, clean start.

> *He who finds a wife finds a good thing,*
> *And obtains favor from the LORD.*
> *—Proverbs 18:22*

CHAPTER 8

Second Chance

Soon after our marriage, my construction company sent me further north in California to oversee some projects. Carla and I picked a small mountain hamlet called Paradise for our new home. We had saved enough money to make a down payment on a cute little house tucked back in the forest.

I cut down on my drinking and came home from work like other married men. There was hunting and fishing right outside my back door. Fresh mountain air and folksy neighbors added to our contentment. Even the gas station attendant took time for a chat while wiping the front windshield. The waitresses at the local coffee shop called us by name.

On Saturdays Carla and I—accompanied by Trouble, our Brittany spaniel— would launch our aluminum boat into Lake Oroville and catch bass all day long. This was life! A good woman, a change of scenery, a faithful bird dog, and a place to call my own was all I needed for happiness.

Apparently, though, Carla didn't feel as euphoric. She began acting strange. I'd catch her staring into space and being some-what distant.

"What's wrong, honey?" I'd ask.

"Oh, nothing," she'd say. "Just thinking, that's all. No big deal."

Now and then she would disappear into the bedroom while I was watching the evening news, and I'd catch her reading her Bible. Occasionally I'd waken at 3:00 in the morning and find her on her knees by the side of the bed, crying and talking softly to God.

What is wrong with this woman? I fretted. *I'm giving her everything she could possibly want. Now what? And why does she need to pray like that? Nighttime is for sleeping.*

I didn't have the heart to tell her that praying was a waste of time. After all, God didn't help me make the basketball team back in the sixth grade, so why would He help her?

Driving to work some mornings, I would think, *What a strange bunch of kinfolks I've got. But they sure seem happy, so maybe they do have something I don't have. I'll just let it slide.*

One night I came home and Carla greeted me at the door, her eyes dancing. "Guess what?" she asked excitedly.

"What?"

"Guess!" she repeated.

"Carla, I'm not in the mood for Twenty Questions. I'm tired, dear. I've had a hard day."

"Sit down," she said. "I have news for you."

"Now what? Are we being audited by the IRS?"

"We're going to have a baby!"

A tidal wave of emotions cascaded through me! Joy. An awareness of responsibility. Fear of change. Then more joy.

"Really?" I blurted out. "When?"

"Around Christmas," beamed my wife.

That night I sat up late thinking. *Dick, you've been given a second chance. Now don't blow this one. You are going to be a father again, and this time you're not a crazy nineteen-year-old. You are almost 32. It's time to grow up and be everything to this child that you are supposed to be—everything that your dad never was to you.*

"THANK YOU, JESUS"

To me, the fall was the best season in Paradise. The trees exploded with brilliant colors of red, orange, and sun-burst yellow. The air became crisp. The sky turned cobalt blue with billowing clouds floating overhead like massive ships. There was a great duck club down in Woodland, about 80 miles south. The reports from the State Department of Fish and Game looked good. I felt excited. Plenty of ducks and geese were flocking to the lakes and fields.

The season began, but I stayed home on weekends with Carla, my sense of loyalty telling me to take care of her. At night I'd sit in front of the roaring fireplace, clean my shotgun and count the shells I had left from the year before. Between sips of coffee I scratched ole Trouble's floppy ears. My dog seemed to sense that his favorite time of year was upon us. He'd sniff my 12-gauge shotgun and wag his tail with anticipation.

Carla, now seven-and-a-half months along, would sit in her favorite chair with her lap full of baby books. "Come feel the baby kicking!" she'd squeal every now and then. I would jump up and lay my hand on her belly. Even after dozens of times, a thrill kept zipping through me.

One weekend toward the end of the season, one of my buddies named Curt called. "Bernal, you should have seen the mallards today," he said. "We didn't even have to use our guns—they just surrendered and landed in the back of the pickups."

"Good-bye, Curt. Thanks for calling, pal," I grumbled, as I hung up on my laughing friend.

"Why don't you go hunting with the guys?" asked Carla. "I'm not going to have the baby yet. If anything happens, I know how to get hold of you."

"You hear that, Trouble?" I asked my dog. He wagged his tail. "We're going hunting, boy!"

That Friday night I drove south and joined the guys at our duck club meeting. We played cards, drank a couple of bottles of brandy, and tapped our toes to country and western music until 1:00 a.m.

The alarm went off at 4:00 a.m. on Saturday morning. I clambered into my gear, feeling the dull pound in my temples of a hangover. We drove out to the blind, camouflaged the dogs, poured ourselves cups of steaming hot coffee, and got our duck calls ready. Just as the sun began to make its morning climb, a flock of ducks appeared high above our pond, looking for a place to land.

My heart pounded with adrenaline. Then I looked across the way. *Who is that nut out there with his pickup lights on? This is private property. No vehicles are allowed. He's scaring all the ducks away. Of all the nerve! Who is that guy?*

"Dick," a familiar voice called out, a shadowy figure approaching through the mist. It was Carl, the dog trainer who got me into the club a few years back. "Her water broke, Dick," he called.

"What?"

"You're about to become a father," Carl announced, as deadpan as ever.

"My gosh!" I hollered as I ran to my truck. "Where is my truck?" *Oh, great. J. W.'s wife borrowed it.* "J. W.," I shouted, "give me your keys, man, quick. Come on, I'm about to be a father!"

Hysterical laughter erupted from each blind. I jumped into J. W.'s old Chevy pickup that would not go more than 60 miles an hour. It took 90 minutes to get to Feather River Hospital.

Completely forgetting that I had on a full set of waders, I waddled straight into the maternity ward—duck calls, hat, shotgun, shells, gloves, and all. When the nurse saw me, she broke into laughter. "He's here!" she yelled to the other nurses.

I didn't find much humor in any of this. As they led me into Carla's room, I felt relieved to see that she had not delivered yet. She was just starting labor.

"Sorry, sweetheart," she grinned. "Didn't mean to mess up your hunting trip."

"Hey, don't worry about it. I'm glad I'm here."

I was starting to feel a little silly about my get-up. The nurse said, "Mr. Bernal, why don't you go on home? It will be hours yet, and her sister is here to keep her company. Go get some rest. You look as if you could use it."

Back home I was too keyed up to sleep. I kept my eye on the phone while doing a few chores. Finally, around 4:30 p.m., the call came.

"It's time, Mr. Bernal," said the nurse.

Carla and I had attended classes on natural childbirth, so I knew what to do when I got there. But while I was coaching Carla, my body realized just how tired it was. I couldn't stop yawning. The doctor saw my fatigue and recommended that I use his office couch to catch a wink or two. He assured me it would be an hour or so before delivery. So Carla, who had been counting on me to coach her through the delivery, had to rely on her sister Karen, while her Prince Charming sawed logs in the office next door.

Finally, the doctor came and shook my shoulder. "It's time, Dick," he announced. I followed him into the room where my wife was huffing and puffing through the final pangs of labor. Feeling somewhat guilty, I tried to help, but there was no time left. In the next instant my baby girl slipped into the world! Carla and I cried openly.

"Sarah. We'll call her Sarah," we agreed.

That night I sat up late with ole Trouble. It felt good to be alive.

I wonder if all that praying Carla did paid off? I asked myself. I was beginning to believe in miracles. I had just witnessed one—a human birth coupled with a supernatural presence. It took more than human effort to create that beautiful baby!

Though weak from the birth, Carla whispered, "Thank you, Jesus," over and over again.

To everything there is a season,
A time to be born.
—Ecclesiastes 3:2

CHAPTER 9

Some Kind of Miracle

A few days after Sarah's birth, I had to work on a job in Sacramento. The carpenter foreman shouted at me from below the wall I was reinforcing. "Hey, Bernal, there's an emergency call for you down in the office."

Oh, no, I thought. *Not the baby, not Sarah.* I tore down to the office and grabbed the phone. "Hello, this is Dick," I said, trying to sound calm.

Karen told me that Carla had been taken back to the hospital for profuse hemorrhaging.

"I'll be right there," I said. I flew out of the office. Paradise seemed a million miles away. My wife needed me as never before. In my frustration, I cursed and beat my fist against the dashboard. I was driving at top speed, yet felt like I was crawling that 100 miles.

A stream of thoughts rushed through my mind. *What am I going to do when I get there? What can I say? What if she is dead?* I suddenly felt angry at that God of hers. Here I was a drinking, smoking, cursing heathen—and I was healthy as a horse. But my poor little wife, who was a God-fearing, Bible-reading woman was bleeding to death.

"It's not fair," I ranted. "It is just not fair!"

I ran every red light and ignored every speed limit sign. When the hospital finally came into sight, I began to tremble with desperation.

Why do people have to die?

Who designed this thing called life?

Why are there so many complications attached to it?

If God's in charge, then why do people suffer?

Dare I pray for Carla?

Would God even listen to someone like me?

At my wits end, I quit thinking and started praying. "God, Jesus, Whoever You are, please help Carla. I beg You, please heal my wife. She truly loves You and talks about You to me. I know I don't deserve an audience with You, but if You can find it in Your heart to do this, I will do whatever You want. I will. I promise. Thank You for hearing me out."

I pulled into the hospital parking lot where a few days before we'd felt unspeakable joy in carrying our baby daughter out to the car. I double-parked and ran to the emergency entrance. I kept telling myself that everything was going to be all right.

Our doctor met me outside Carla's room. I could tell by his expression that things were not going well.

"Dick, we've got a major problem," he said. He explained that a piece of the placenta had not been expelled after Sarah's birth. Ten days later, when it had broken loose, it had torn a main artery. They couldn't seem to stop the hemorrhaging. They had already done a dilation and curettage procedure. Now they were thinking of a complete hysterectomy.

Carla looked horrible when I walked into her room. Yellow skin. Chalk white lips. She looked like a corpse. Nurses were working frantically to get her blood pressure up, but it was steadily dropping.

She came to enough to whisper in my ear. "I'm sorry, honey."

Wanting to give reassurance, I patted her gently on the head. "Don't worry, you're going to be fine. What are you sorry for, anyway? It's not your fault."

On the doctor's orders, I left the hospital room and drove to Karen's house. She was looking after Sarah. I felt an incredible fatherly urge to hold my daughter. I cuddled little Sarah in a rocking chair and chucked her under the chin. "Your mom is in a bit of a jam right now," I whispered. "What do you think about all this? Do you think it's going to be okay? Yeah, I think so, too. Boy, I wish I could be as peaceful as you are right now."

Every time the phone rang, I flinched, wanting to answer it, yet afraid of what I might hear. News had spread to family and friends in the Bay Area, so the calls were coming in fast and furious. Even my crusty iron working buddies were calling, concern showing in their voices. They offered help, money, and even their own blood if necessary. The next voice I heard was the doctor's, saying that they were going to decide on the hysterectomy in the morning.

I hardly slept at all. The next morning, Karen and I anxiously waited outside Carla's room for the news. Silently and hardly breathing, I repeated my promise to God.

The doctor walked out of Carla's room and turned to us. He was beaming. "We seem to have some kind of miracle here," he said. "Last night, the blood flow suddenly stopped. I can't explain it, but I can tell you that we have a rapidly recovering young woman on our hands, and she's very hungry."

I raced into the room. There was my wife smiling and sitting up.

Let us therefore come boldly to the throne of grace,
that we may obtain mercy and find grace to help in time of need.
—Hebrews 4:16

Kingdom Journey

CHAPTER 10

Joy In Heaven

I drove down to the Feather River Hospital to pick up Carla on Christmas Eve. Walking across the parking lot toward the hospital entrance, I stopped, gazed up at the stars, and said out loud, "Thank You, God."

I felt good saying thank you, but then I remembered my impulsive promise to God. "If You will heal Carla, I will do anything You ask of me," I had vowed.

What on earth can God do with me? I puzzled. *Nothing. I'm not in His league.* I shrugged my shoulders and walked on. I purposely didn't tell Carla about my deal with God. I knew she took God seriously, and I didn't want her to use my promise as leverage to get me into a church.

For the next several weeks, I tried to get back into my usual routine—work, family, and a few beers to ease the tensions. But I kept thinking about God. *Who is God, anyway? Why is there a God? Where did He come from?* I would catch myself staring at the sky and wondering about the place called heaven.

One clear Saturday in January, toward the end of duck season, I sat in my blind watching the geese and ducks migrate south. *Why do they do that? Is there really a God who controls nature? Even this ant crawling across my boot seems to have a purpose in life. Amazing! I wonder where I fit in.*

That Friday I came home to the aroma of my favorite stew. "Hope you're hungry, honey," said Carla. "I made this specially for you."

"Great," I said. "I'm famished. Listen, dear, I am going to the club in the morning. It's the last week of duck season. But I'll come home tomorrow night, and we can go to church Sunday morning. What do you say?"

"Really? Honest? Oh, honey, this is great. God has answered my prayers."

I hope she understands I'm not going to make a habit of it, I thought. *I just want to make good on my promise to God by showing up once in His house.*

On Sunday morning I stood in front of my closet looking over my limited wardrobe. *What do people wear to church?* I wondered. My collection of work and hunting/fishing attire did not include any Sunday go-to-meeting suits. My eyes fell on my Tom Jones style lightning-blue jumpsuit. *That'll look nice.* I put it on even though it fit a little tight. *What else?* I thought. *Oh yes—how about this electric green Elvis Presley shirt. Perfect. I'll unbutton the top to show off my gold chain and cross.* I completed the ensemble with a pair of Tony Lama ostrich skin boots.

Carla was so excited that she could care less how I looked. Little Sarah was very pretty in a new pink dress.

Carla had spotted a nice little denominational church, so that is where we went. As we walked in, I noticed a lot of older folks. I had always loved senior citizens, probably because of my great respect for my grandparents. The gentleman next to me was really old, maybe 90. His eyes were closed and his head lay back in an unorthodox position for church. In fact, he looked dead. I watched him for a long time wondering, *Is this guy breathing?*

After a few songs out of a book they called a hymnal, the

preacher started in. He was a nice, safe-looking man who seemed at peace with himself. He spoke of God's goodness and mercy as if he really knew all about it first hand. About halfway through the message, the old man next to me snorted out loud and took a deep breath. I almost jumped out of my skin, but I was very relieved to know he was alive.

Carla thought I wasn't too impressed with the service. After we were dismissed, she began inquiring about any nearby churches with people closer to our ages. A sweet little old lady suggested a church of another denomination that was right up the road. She said that we would find a much younger congregation.

"Well?" Carla asked, as we started for home. "What did you think?"

"I liked it," I said. "It felt good."

Somewhat surprised but encouraged, she pressed her advantage and said, "How about next Sunday? Do you want to try the other church?"

"Sure," I replied. "Why not?" Actually, I had gotten excited about this new adventure of hunting for God, but I wasn't going to let her see my enthusiasm.

The next Sunday we drove into the packed parking lot of a large, impressive looking church. Carla carried Sarah in, saying, "Here, hold my Bible while I find the nursery."

Man, it felt strange to carry a Bible. I felt a little embarrassed—like I do when I'm holding my wife's purse and she's trying on dresses. *Won't everybody stare at me?* Then I saw several men carrying Bibles. That helped me out a little.

A big, rough-looking guy stood in the church doorway shaking hands with everyone who passed. *How about that?* I thought. *Churches even have doormen.*

"Now, who do we have here?" he asked as we entered the lobby.

My wife answered. "I'm Carla, this is little Sarah, and this is my husband, Dick."

Before I knew it, his big hand had grabbed mine. "What do you do for a living, Dick?"

"I'm a rod buster," I responded. "We're remodeling the State Capitol Building."

"An ironworker!" he barked. "I don't like ironworkers. I'm a carpenter."

I just stared at him until he broke into a belly laugh. His laughter subsided into a warm smile and he patted me on the back. I felt genuinely welcomed to church by this man's man.

"I like that guy," I whispered to Carla. We found seats and listened to the choir and some announcements. For the next forty minutes, I sat mesmerized by the words coming from a handsome, silver-haired pastor. He talked about how people could make a U-turn from self-centered living to a life of trusting God and serving others. He said that God sent His Son Jesus into the world to make friends with us and save us from sin and hell. I began to perspire. I couldn't escape the fact that the pastor was inviting me to come face to face with God and own up to the way I'd been living.

The pastor closed by asking everyone to bow their heads and close their eyes. I wanted to make a beeline for the men's room. Anything to get out of there. Next the pastor asked if there was anyone who would like to come down to the altar to accept Jesus into their hearts. My body froze, as if paralyzed, because I realized that the choice was mine.

Carla was affected differently. She jumped to her feet. "Come on, honey, let's go," she exclaimed as she grabbed my arm. She tried to pull me out into the aisle. "Let's go, Dick!"

"What are you doing, woman?" I said a bit too loud. "Let go of my arm!"

I felt my face heating up. The people around us were smiling and nodding as if to say, "Do it. Go to the altar with your wife."

Carla got miffed by my bullheadedness. "Well, I'm going by myself," she said, and off she headed up the aisle toward the preacher.

I felt totally exposed before the whole world. I watched a lady counselor take Carla to a back room. All kinds of thoughts began rushing through my mind. *What were they doing to her back there? What is she saying to them?* I had read about weird cults that entrapped people. I thought about finding Sarah and running out of the building.

Just then, Carla appeared from a side door, beaming from ear to ear. She walked back to our aisle and hugged me. "I did it, honey," she said. "I rededicated my life to Jesus. I feel great. I wish you had come with me."

"I suppose you gave our house away and all our savings," I said, trying to put a damper on things.

"Oh, don't be silly," she smiled. "I've never been so happy."

That afternoon I sat in our living room quietly pondering all I had heard and seen. Carla was busy in the kitchen, cooking and talking baby talk to Sarah. She was extremely happy. Apparently knowing what was going on in my mind, she walked out and dropped a book into my lap.

"What's this?" I asked, puzzled by the cover.

"It's called the *Wordless Book*. It's all colors. There is a message on the back page that explains the meaning. Check it out, sweetheart."

It was an odd-looking book. There were colored pages: black, gold, red, and white. There were no words on the pages. I flipped to the back page and read an explanation. The black page was man's life without God—sinful and ugly. The gold page represented God's purity and holiness. The red page signified the blood of Jesus Christ that takes away our sin. And the white page represented a person whose sins have been cleansed by the blood of the Lamb. A little prayer for salvation followed.

I looked through the book once more. I remembered my awareness in church that the choice was mine. I made an inner decision and slowly spoke out loud the prayer for salvation: "Dear God, I acknowledge that I have followed my own way and that I am a sinner. I ask You to forgive me and to accept the blood of Your Son Jesus Christ as an eternal sacrifice for my sin. Please accept me into Your family and guide me all the days of my life. In Jesus' name, Amen."

For the next few minutes I stared out of the window into

the backyard. I studied our big olive tree, its branches gently swaying in the afternoon breeze. I'm not quite sure what I expected to happen. A feeling, perhaps. Or maybe a heavenly voice congratulating me. Or an angelic choir praising my decision to take the plunge. But the truth was that I simply felt light and happy.

A heavy load had been lifted off me. I couldn't explain it, but for the first time in my life, I felt truly free.

"Carla," I called softly.

Carla came into the living room, drying a dinner plate. "What's wrong, honey?"

"Well, I did it," I said.

"You did what?" she asked.

"This." I held up the book. "I said the prayer at the end of the little book you gave me. I'm saved—isn't that what you call it? Saved? Getting saved?"

I don't know how much excitement ripples through heaven when a person comes to Christ. But if it rivals the goings-on at Rosewood Lane that second Sunday afternoon in February 1977, in the town of Paradise, California, then it must be all-out wonderful.

Carla burst into tears of joy, jumped around like a little girl, clapped her hands, and thanked our Jesus for bringing her husband into God's own family.

I say to you that likewise there will be more joy in heaven over one sinner who repents than over ninety-nine just persons who need no repentance.
—Luke 15:7

CHAPTER 11

The Family of God

After the spontaneous celebration of my new spiritual life, Carla seized the moment. "Let's pray for something right now," she insisted.

Usually, when she got in one of those strong moods, I would rebel, but not today. She was no longer just my wife. She was now a sister in the Lord who knew a whole lot more about what was going on than I did.

"Okay," I said. "Pray for what?"

"Let's ask the Lord to take away your desire for cigarettes. Honey, please, I hate the smell of those nasty things, especially when we kiss. It'll make kissing more romantic and you'll stay alive longer!"

"Well, sure, let's go for it," I said, trying to be brave. "But you do the praying."

Carla prayed with all her heart. And to my absolute astonishment, my craving for nicotine instantly vanished. I felt awe for a Creator who loves, hears, and helps us humans. To think I had

57

lived 32 years without knowing that! Why hadn't anyone told me about this wonderful God before? And why hadn't someone told my dad, so that he could have found happiness, instead of being so tormented?

At work the next week in Sacramento, I told everyone about the change in my life. My friends laughed at first, thinking it was a joke. Then they realized I was serious. One by one the guys began to avoid me. Boy, that hurt!

I had counted on these men as my partners for life, buddies who would stick with me through thick and thin. Why couldn't they understand and be happy for me? I still loved them. Why were they acting as if I had the plague? Was it because I didn't smoke, get drunk, or cuss like a sailor anymore?

But I quit blaming them. After all, how could they understand the change I had gone through? I remembered all too well the years I had known nothing about God's love. I decided to ease up. I would still be their friend and see if they could come around. Why couldn't we still go hunting and fishing together, and have a good time?

A short time later we were all working on a job near Calistoga. The new bumper sticker on my truck read, "Jesus loves you." During lunch break, someone mentioned the bumper sticker. One by one, my long-time friends took pot shots at my new-found faith. I tried to be a sport about it, but it really hurt. Why all the antagonism?

That evening, as I drove back across the valley toward Paradise, I came to a conclusion. Things would never be the same. I had to either return to my old way of life to please my friends, or go all the way with Jesus and lose them. There wasn't room for compromise.

I had many fond memories of my friends, my carefree way of living, and all that went with it. But none of that compared to the new life in Christ I had found. Though I had broken more than a few promises with no sense of guilt, I wanted to keep the promise I had made to God the night He miraculously healed Carla. I had no idea what His plans were for me, but I decided to find out.

Two elderly gentlemen came to our home to talk about joining the church. Fired up by my recent decision, I jumped in with both feet. The next Sunday when the pastor gave an altar call, I walked down the aisle and made a public commitment to follow Jesus.

Afterwards, the associate pastor took me into the counseling room and asked me a strange question. "Dick, where is Jesus now?"

"In heaven," I replied, trying to sound correct.

"Yes, that is true," the minister said with a smile. "But where is He in Dick Bernal's life?"

"Oh, uh, in my heart," I answered, desperately wanting to say the right thing.

The man nodded, apparently satisfied. At the end of the counseling session, I went to ask the senior pastor a question. I was guarded about my secret covenant with the Lord over Carla's ordeal, so I phrased my question this way: "Sir, I feel God wants me to do something for Him. But you see, I have a, well—interesting past. I haven't exactly lived according to the Bible. You might even say I was a real sinner, if you get my drift."

Sensing my struggle to bare my soul, the minister reached for his Bible and found a passage. "Dick, listen to this," he said: "Therefore if any man is in Christ, he is a new creature; the old things passed away; behold, new things have come" (2 Cor. 5:17). Then he asked me to read the passage back to him. I did so.

"This is God's Word, Dick," he continued. "God's Word is truth. God's Word is His will, and God says you don't have a sinful past anymore, only a glorious future. You can do anything God asks of you if you are willing."

I left the session practically glowing. On the way home, I contemplated our conversation. *Can this be true?* I wondered. *Are all those ugly, selfish things I did forgotten because of the blood of Jesus? Did God take a heavenly eraser and wipe out the sins of my youth? Am I completely forgiven for all the people I hurt and used? Boy, I want to believe this, but it seems too good to be true!*

Dick Bernal

HERE I AM!

The church bulletin mentioned a clean-up day the following Saturday. I thought maybe I could contribute something as a skilled construction worker and crew foreman. That Saturday at 8:00 a.m., I was the first one there, work clothes on and coffee in hand. A man with a smile on his face approached me. He held out his hand, shook mine, and introduced himself as Bill.

"Who do we have here?" he asked.

"I'm Dick," I said. "I'm new at church."

"Have you come to work?" he asked.

"Yes, sir. I'm reporting for duty. What are we doing today?"

"Oh, just the general things, you know. Cleaning up, pulling weeds, a little painting here and there, and a little roof repair."

"I'm pretty handy," I said.

Bill disappeared into the shed and came back with a large broom. "Here's a good place to start. We need the sidewalk swept."

The sidewalk swept? I said to myself. So there I was, sweeping the sidewalk for Jesus.

I was halfway done when I heard a familiar honk from an old pickup. My fishing buddy, Jim, was heading down to the local tavern for a few beers and a little pool.

He pulled over and stuck his head out the window. "Hey, Dick, what are you doing? Serving time?"

"No," I said, "Just helping out a little."

"Helping out? Hey, forget that nonsense. Let's go have some fun!"

"No thanks, Jim," I said. "There's more to be done here at the church."

He stared at me for a moment, shook his head, and drove on. I saw him crane his neck to peer at me in the rear view mirror. *Does he think I'm nuts?*

A little later, the tough-looking man who had greeted me at the church walked up. "Hey, Dick, you ready for a little refreshment?"

"Sure," I said, picturing the beers that Jim had offered.

"What'll it be?" the man offered. "Tea or lemonade?"

Tea or lemonade, I thought. *My gosh, what had I gotten myself into?*

But it wasn't long before Carla and I began to really like our new church home. We attended a Young Marrieds Class every Sunday morning before the service. On Tuesday nights, we enjoyed a home Bible study with five other couples. The sting of rejection from my former friends was eased by the caring I experienced with my new church family—the family of God.

I will be a Father to you,
And you shall be My sons and daughters,
Says the LORD Almighty.
2 Corinthians 6:18

CHAPTER 12

Baby Christians Can Be Dangerous

One Sunday morning after the service, Pastor Bob, who was in charge of visitation, asked if I would like to learn how to witness.

"Witness?" I asked. "You mean talking to people about God? I don't think I'm quite ready for that, Pastor Bob."

The next day at work, I tried to picture myself witnessing and talking to people about the Lord. It might not be all that hard if only I knew what to say. The following night Carla and I showed up at the Evangelism and Visitation class. Pastor Bob taught from a little yellow booklet called *The Four Spiritual Laws.* The principles he discussed made sense to me and seemed simple enough to share with others.

Bob separated us into teams of two, pairing seasoned veterans with newcomers. Then he told each team to visit a family who had attended our church for the first time. After a word of prayer from our fearless leader, we all left with assignments in hand.

My cohort gently knocked on the door of an attractive split-level home. When I heard footsteps, I took a half-step backward. I didn't feel all that confident.

The door jerked open and a man eyed us suspiciously. "What do you want?" he bellowed. I noticed a highball in the man's hand and smelled whiskey in the air.

"Hello, sir," replied my associate. "We're from the church you attended last week. May we come in and talk to you about Jesus?"

"Ethel, come here," the man yelled.

Poor Ethel came to the door. It was obvious that she, too, had partaken of more than her share of alcoholic libation. Then old "red eyes" barked at her.

"I told you not to fill out that stupid card at the church! Now look. Here they are on the doorstep!"

"Calm down, dear," pleaded Ethel. "These nice men are just trying to do their job."

"I want to tell you two something," her husband declared. "I liked your church until that phony-baloney, silver-tongued car salesman started all that garbage about salvation. Then I wanted to vomit," he roared.

His face got as red as his eyes, and he began poking me in the chest. The more he raised his voice, the more I forgot why we were there. Here I was trying to be longsuffering as befitted a Christian. But the man got louder and uglier by the second. Suddenly, my patience snapped like a twig.

I grabbed him by the throat and dragged him out on the front lawn, intending to pound him to a pulp. Ethel was screaming her head off for the police. When my partner tried to pull me off of the man, I threatened him and Ethel both.

When the man started gagging in my arms, it dawned on me that I was choking the man I had come to save. I let go of him and ran for the car, crying, "Oh, Jesus, what have I done?" I broke into tears, knowing I'd really blown it. Certainly now God would throw me out of His kingdom. I hadn't changed at all. I was the same old Dick Bernal.

A wave of despair flooded my soul. *God, I can't live this*

life, I prayed. *I'm sorry, but I'm just not cut out to be a Christian.*

My partner didn't say a word as he drove us back to the church. I was dreading facing the pastor. He had placed a lot of faith in me. And Carla would be so embarrassed. I died a thousand deaths as we turned into the church parking lot.

Looking around, I thought, *Great! Everyone else is already back.*

My teammate took the pastor off to one side and began whispering to him. Carla was all smiles as her partner reported that they had led a woman to God. The other teams congratulated Carla for a job well done.

My wife then looked at me. "How did you do, honey?" she asked.

"You don't want to know, believe me," I whispered.

"Why? What's wrong?"

Just then the pastor walked up. "I tell you what, Dick," he said, "next week how about you working with me?"

"Next week?" I asked, feeling my eyes moisten with tears. "You mean you want me to come back?"

"Sure," he said. "One little setback can't stop the work of the Lord, now can it, Dick? Go on home. Everything is going to be fine. See you Sunday at church."

Pastor Bob's love and understanding kept me in the church. During the next few months, I begged God to forgive me so many times that I'm sure He got weary of my pleas. I hope that some loving believer has repaired the damage I caused to poor Ethel and her husband.

Because of ignorance or lack of discipline, baby Christians can be dangerous. Yet I found out that there is room for Dick Bernal in the kingdom of God.

If we confess our sins,
He is faithful and just to forgive us our sins
and to cleanse us from all unrighteousness.
—1 John 1:9

CHAPTER 13

Who Are These Crazy People?

Over the next year and a half, Carla and I became fixtures around the church. We attended barbecues, volleyball games, young-married get-togethers, and church services. I really looked forward to our home group meeting every Tuesday night. Even though most of the group were retired folks, I grew attached to each of them. I even worked up short teachings on the Bible. But Carla began to get that far away, hungry look again.

Work was slow during the summer of 1978, so I spent more time at home. Carla kept talking about a couple of Bible teachers on the local Christian radio station.

"Honey, you have to listen to these guys. Please listen! They really are wonderful, and each program is only fifteen min-utes long."

I finally gave in, wondering what could they tell me that I hadn't already heard. The speaker on the first program talked about the authority the Christian has in the name of Jesus. He spoke of healing and casting out demons as if both should be available to believers today. I was interested in the message.

We sat and listened to another fifteen minutes by a preacher interviewing a farmer from Arkansas about how faith could be used in hunting and fishing. *Man, I like these guys!* I thought. They made the point that a believer should use faith in every aspect of life.

Listening to these preachers became a daily habit. They had a way of presenting the Word in a very practical fashion. I grew to cherish those little fifteen-minute broadcasts on Monday through Friday.

That August, we heard of an upcoming convention in Anaheim, California. We decided to take the week off and see for ourselves what the "faith business" was all about.

When we entered the conference center, I was shocked to see more than four thousand people standing with their hands raised in praise to the Lord. We sat down in seats located behind the speaker. As I looked around at the huge crowd, I found myself going into a trance. I had a vision, seeing myself standing before even bigger crowds and preaching the gospel. The vision gave way to an inner voice which said, "Yea, you will certainly stand in front of bigger crowds and preach My name."

Returning to what was going on around me, I noticed that people were swaying back and forth, singing in a foreign language I had never heard before. I remembered the day my friends and I had gotten spooked when we sneaked into a "holy rollers" meeting back in Watsonville. The singing continued for several minutes. I was shocked to see Carla joining right in with these lunatics! There she stood with her hands raised and eyes closed, with what sounded to me like gibberish coming from her lips.

She had mentioned experiencing the baptism of the Holy Spirit, but I had never heard her pray in tongues before. *Who needs all this, anyway?* I thought. *Why don't they just sing regular hymns and pray in English?*

Finally, one of the preachers came out and began expounding on Ephesians. He shouted, jumped up and down, and even stuck his tongue out in a "raspberry" at those caught in religious traditions.

He is really quite funny, I thought. And I admitted to myself that he was effective in his point that believers needed all the faith they could muster. Towards the end of the service, he asked if anyone needed hands laid on them for healing.

Hands laid on them? Does he mean like in the Bible? Does this guy think he is Jesus or something? We don't lay hands on people in our church. What is the purpose in that anyway?

Hundreds of people streamed toward the front of the auditorium. There were so many that the ushers lined them up around the walls of the huge room. The preacher paused to announce that the Lord had just spoken to him about a particular infirmity.

Oh, wonderful! I thought. *Now God is talking to this guy in person. No wonder my pastors have warned me about Pentecostals.*

"God wants to heal people here with heart problems!" declared the preacher.

"Go on, honey, get prayed for," Carla begged.

"Shhh, I'm fine, sweetheart, really. There's no problem with me. I'm okay." But she was well aware of the history of the Bernal men: heart attacks took my father and his brother, Harry, early in life. And I suffered from occasional dizziness and heart palpitations.

"Please go on up there," she pressed. "What can it hurt?"

Seeing I wasn't going to win this one with Carla, and fascinated by it all, I found a place and squeezed in line. As I stood there, I saw people falling over backwards. Ushers would stand behind and catch them, easing them to the carpet.

How come they're falling? I asked myself. *He's not hitting them. He's just touching their foreheads. Is this the power of God at work?*

Before I knew it the preacher was next to me. "Be healed, in Jesus' name," he shouted as he touched the person directly in front of me. I wondered if he had ever watched Oral Roberts on television years ago as I had. Just then, I felt his hand on my forehead.

Instantly, I felt as if the top of my head opened up and a breath of cool air was flowing into my body. I glanced up to see if an air conditioner had been turned on above me. Then I realized the feeling was inside my body, not outside. *How odd.* I made my way back to my seat, my body feeling light and airy.

"What did he say?" asked Carla. "What did you feel?"

Before I could answer, the song leader asked everyone to stand and worship the Lord. Nearly every person in the room lifted their hands and began to sing in the Spirit, as they called it.

Feeling left out, I thought, *Oh, what the heck! Go ahead, Bernal, lift your hands, a little bit anyway. It's not going to kill you. Besides, no one from our church is here to see.*

I bravely lifted my arms a few inches, feeling as if weights of self-consciousness were attached to them. As everyone around me was spontaneously praising the Lord, I opened my mouth and gibberish came out! I tried again with the same result. It sounded like baby talk. I began to laugh at my dilemma. Carla asked what was wrong.

"Every time I try to praise God in English, I can't!" I complained.

"You've got it!" she screamed.

"Got what?"

"Honey, you've received the baptism of the Holy Spirit and your new prayer language. You can speak in tongues now."

"Wait a minute," I said. "I'm not sure I want this. I didn't ask for it. What is my church going to think? Me, a tongue-talker?" But nothing could take away my wife's joy.

That night and the next morning Carla put her ear on my chest to listen to my heart. The irregularity of the heartbeat was gone. The rhythm was strong and normal. A physical confirmed the healing that had occurred. Since that summer of 1978, my heartbeat has been absolutely perfect.

As we drove home to Paradise from the Charismatic Convention, I knew somehow that our lives would never be the same.

Soon after, Carla located a small group of Charismatics who

met at 2:00 each Sunday afternoon. Charismatics are Christians who believe that God still does miracles through the power of the Holy Spirit and the Word of God. Whether they are called Charismatic or Pentecostal, these believers attest to the presence of healing, visions, prophesy, spiritual gifts, and praying in tongues in the Body of Christ today.

The leader of the group Carla found was a former Roman Catholic priest named Vincent O'Shaughnessy. The church was called Paradise Christian Center.

As much as Carla loved our own church and all the new friends we had made, she felt inwardly prompted to become involved in Paradise Christian Center. However, there was one major road block—me!

I was not about to leave our first church.

For he who speaks in a tongue does not speak to men but to God,
for no one understands him; however,
in the spirit he speaks mysteries.
—1 Corinthians 14:2

Dick Bernal

CHAPTER 14

Man With A Mission

On the second Sunday of October 1978, northern California was enjoying a beautiful Indian summer. After church, Carla started in on me again. "Please, sweetheart, come with me to hear Pastor Vince tonight," she begged. "You'll love his teaching. He's talking about the gifts of the Spirit."

I don't know if it was the glorious weather, the fact that the Raiders had won that day, or the knowledge that duck season was only a week away, but I was in a very good mood. "Sure, why not?" I agreed. "Let's go."

Walking up the steps to the church doors, we could hear music and singing. The pastor stood by the door greeting latecomers. "Hi, Carla, and this must be Dick," smiled the friendly man of God.

A slight Irish brogue complimented his warm manner and distinguished looks. Once everyone was seated, the pastor began teaching. I counted about twenty people. I felt sorry for them, reasoning that it must be hard to start a church with no help from a denomination. But they seemed happy and full of love.

Bernal, turn off your brain and listen to what the man has to say. You might learn something.

"This evening," he said, "I am going to talk about why you should speak in tongues."

Carla glanced at me with one of those wifely looks that says, "Boy, do you ever need to hear this!"

I had decided not to pursue my brief experience of praying in tongues at the Anaheim convention. Praying in tongues wasn't accepted in our denomination. Looking back, I believe that I was quenching the Holy Spirit.

Now as Pastor Vince was speaking, I noticed that everything he said was backed up with Scripture. For the next hour, Pastor Vince threaded together a scriptural precedence for the gifts of the Holy Spirit—healing, visions, prophesy, singing and praying in tongues. He drew from Isaiah, Acts, and Corinthians. I like the continuity of the Old and New Testaments. He concluded that the signs and wonders of the first century are still available for believers today.

I was amazed that the Word of God so clearly spoke of spiritual gifts as instrumental in building up the body of Christ and overcoming the powers of darkness.

As he brought the message to a close, Pastor Vince paused for a moment as if hearing an unseen voice. Then he said, "I believe someone here needs God's power in his life, someone needs the baptism of the Holy Spirit." Dear Lord, he was looking right at me!

"Yes, praise God!" Carla shouted loudly. "Amen."

There she goes again, I thought, *answering for me.* But at that moment an inner voice echoed her sentiment. "Yes, Dick, Pastor Vince is talking about you. You need more of My power in your life. You need to receive all that I have for you."

Hesitantly, I stood up and walked forward to the altar. Before I knew it, I was surrounded by other men who laid hands on my shoulders and prayed for me. I felt deeply supported in my quest to draw closer to God.

"Dick, relax and let God move through you," coached Pastor Vince. "Let this happen easily. Give the Holy Spirit your vocal cords."

A quiet flow of power from within began to fill my mouth. People prayed softly for me. I could hear Carla weeping tears of joy. I took a deep breath and exhaled. A rush of foreign words and sounds came streaming out of me. I sounded as if I were speaking an Oriental language. I raised my hands in praise and laughed with joy.

What do you know, I thought. *I can do it! I am not making this up—I feel the power of God flowing through me!*

Needless to say, the people in that little church got real happy that Indian summer night. After we got home, Carla and I stayed up until dawn, praying out loud, laughing at my strange new prayer language, and loving this awesome God of ours. My faith felt turbocharged.

The next morning, tired and blurry-eyed, I drove down the hill toward Sacramento. "Dick," said a voice so clearly that it startled me, "prepare yourself for service, for I have called you."

"Who said that?" I asked out loud. *Was that me? Boy, I should have gotten some sleep last night. I am hearing things!*

"Lord, is that you?" I asked.

The voice came again, repeating, "Dick, prepare yourself for service, for I have called you." I could not tell if the voice was audible or coming from deep within me.

"Okay, Lord, you've got me," I answered. "Let's get on with it." My willingness to obey surprised me.

For the first time in my life, and with a confidence that I still find incredible to believe, I had become a man with a mission.

> *But you shall receive power*
> *when the Holy Spirit has come upon you;*
> *and you shall be witnesses to Me in Jerusalem,*
> *and in all Judea and Samaria,*
> *and to the end of the earth.*
> *—Acts 1:8*

PART TWO:

ESTABLISHING THE KINGDOM

But seek first the kingdom of God

and His righteousness,

and all these things shall be added to you.

—Matthew 6:33

Dick Bernal

CHAPTER 15

Midwest Adventure

It didn't take me long to figure out that if God was going to use me, I needed some training.

After a good deal of prayer, Carla and I decided to attend a Bible College in Tulsa, Oklahoma. But could I give up the security of my union job as an ironworker? Would we starve to death, or was God truly guiding us into a new phase of life and ministry?

God encouraged this drastic change by giving me an unforgettable dream. In the dream I was standing inside a huge building with a red-tiled roof, preaching to thousands of people in San Jose, California. My family and friends were in the congregation. It was a wild, vivid scene. Carla interpreted the dream as a prophetic vision that would surely come true.

The doors quickly opened for us to leave California. We rented our house to a nice family, and gave away most of our belongings—even my boat and most of my precious sporting goods. Giving my dog away brought a lump to my throat, but we could not take him with us. He would be much happier hunting birds with my friends from work.

Saying good-bye to friends and family, we packed all of our earthly belongings inside the little station wagon, and headed off for our midwest adventure.

After a couple of days we pulled up to Carla's aunt's home in Tulsa. The wagon seemed to say, "Enough! Stop! I'm not going another mile." When I stepped out into the 90 degree evening air, reality settled in. *Man,* I thought, *I'm already getting homesick for the cool mountain air of Paradise.*

The next day we visited a friend's sister and brother-in-law. Richard Cardoza had just graduated from the Bible School we'd enrolled in, so he and his wife Corrine gave us the lowdown on school life. We bombarded them with dozens of questions about the strange new environment. That Sunday, they took us to a church that showed me how traditional my church had been in California.

My pastors in California were silver-haired, middle-aged, and soft-spoken. The two Tulsa pastors were cut from a different mold! One looked as if he could play linebacker for the Raiders. His associate reminded me of a young Conway Twitty. The service was alive with enthusiasm. Carla and I savored every moment, watching how God used these two preachers in supernatural ways. We decided to make this our new church home while in Tulsa.

That first Sunday, a missionary was raising money for a gospel tent to be used in India. We were pinching pennies until I could find work, but I could not resist the prompting to give $100 to help those missionaries buy the tent. India had always fascinated me. Now I had an opportunity to bless that nation. Little did I know that three years later, I would preach in Guntur, India— under the very tent I had helped to purchase!

That week we moved into a nice, affordable apartment six miles from campus. During the first few days of school I realized how out of shape I was academically. I had never been much good at reading, studying, and taking notes. My prayer life greatly intensified!

We used what money we had to furnish our little apartment and make the down payment on our tuition. I felt awkward after 13 years of steady employment as an ironworker to be scanning the "help wanted" ads. School hours were from 8:00 a.m. to noon. My only alternatives for working were swing or night shifts.

My first week of job hunting proved futile. I was overqualified for most positions. The second week found us with $12 to our name, after rent and groceries. Driving home from another job rejection, I felt like my chest was in the grip of a giant vise. I pulled over to the side of the road and cried out to God for help.

I walked into our apartment still feeling raw. "Sit down, honey," insisted my wife. "Are you ready for some news?"

"What, dear, ready for what?" I asked. "It better be good news. I've had a really bad morning."

"Well, I'm pregnant," smiled my wife.

Pregnant! God! How could you let this happen to me now? I cried out inside.

A little voice deep down inside whispered, "Son, you reap what you sow."

Yeah, Lord, I know. But what about the timing? Here I sit with less than $12 in my wallet. Bible school bills are piling up, the rent is coming due, and my wife is pregnant.

When I grumbled about our finances, my eternally optimistic wife assured me that according to Matthew 6:33, God would take care of us. "Seek first the kingdom of God and His righteousness, and all these things shall be added to you."

Boy, I thought, *I hate it when she quotes the Word to me just when I want to wallow in self-pity. It kind of takes the fun out of it.*

The next afternoon I got in the car and prayed, "God, I'll do anything. Just get me a job, please."

The Lord took me at my word. He got me work in a convenience store.

"Mr. Bernal," said the manager, "you can start tomorrow night. Your hours are from 11 p.m. to 7 a.m. Starting pay is $3.99 an hour. If you work hard, you'll get a 15 cent raise in 90 days.

Here is your shirt—a large size should do the trick."

Can you believe it? Me? Working at the Git-N-Go convenience store for $3.99 an hour? *If my friends could see me now in my cute little orange shirt, they would fall over laughing. I am either called of God or one crazy fool.*

Over the next months, life consisted of school, homework, church, and sleeping now and then. I worked overtime 20 to 30 hours a week just to get by.

FISH OUT OF WATER

I found myself getting self-conscious when Carla and I tried to fellowship with our new found friends. Too often the conversation would drift around to awkward personal topics. "How many kids do you have?" "Where did you meet?" "Are your parents in ministry?" Everyone seemed to assume that this was my first marriage and that I had come from a fine Christian home. Wrong.

I felt like a second class Christian, ashamed that I couldn't speak of a wonderful childhood with God-fearing parents. If I had been totally honest, I would have said, "Oh, Carla and I have two children. I have another son back home with my ex-wife. My dad was a drunk and a womanizer. I've done my fair share of drinking, drugging, and fighting."

But over time I have come to understand that many people who come to love and serve God—both in Biblical times and today—are chosen by Him precisely because of their human flaws and needs.

Even though I felt like a fish out of water, I knew Carla and I were at the right place at the right time doing the right thing. Deep inside I knew that God's call on our lives was based upon His grace, not upon anything I had ever done or not done.

The Christmas season came. A fellow student named Mike Behr brought us a free Christmas tree. You would have thought it was a check for a million dollars. Here we had practically nothing, yet were filled with happiness that Christmas.

A GIT-N-GO COMMUNION

My job soon became a ministry of sorts. Working the grave-yard shift gave me the opportunity to share Jesus with a lot of lonely people. I told my customers all the exciting things I was learning at school. Some were very interested, but others mocked and scoffed. A few even complained to the manager about the preacher at Git-N-Go. He called me on the carpet for witnessing.

But how could I stop telling people that their lives would be wonderful if they accepted Jesus as Lord? One night I was talking to my little congregation of regulars: two homosexuals from the porno shop, a biker's girlfriend with tattoos on both arms, a truck driver, and a bag lady. After preaching to them about how Christ died for their sins so that they could enter the kingdom of God, I led them all in the sinner's prayer. Then I had a zany idea.

"Hey, let's have communion," I said.

"Sure!" they chorused.

"Grab that grape juice on the shelf and a box of saltine crackers," I instructed them. "I'll put it on my tab."

What a sight. My first congregation! I used styrofoam cups to pass around the symbolic blood of Christ, shed for the remission of our sins. And I gave each person a saltine cracker, representing the body of Christ, broken so that they could receive eternal life. I understood as never before that God is reaching out to all people—that Jesus came into the world not to condemn us, but that the world through Him might be saved. I'll never forget the tears in the truck driver's eyes as he reached out with a grimy hand and tenderly received the bread of life.

And Jesus said to them,
I am the bread of life.
He who comes to Me shall never hunger,
and he who believes in Me shall never thirst.
—John 6:35

CHAPTER 16

A New Son

By April Carla was eight months pregnant. Her parents were visiting us for the weekend, when a spring storm with tornado warnings moved in from the south. The crack of lightning and the boom of thunder periodically interrupted our conversation in the living room   As the afternoon wore on, Carla felt increasingly uncomfortable.

"Could it be time for the baby?" asked her mother.

The baby was not due for five weeks. But when Carla's abdominal pains intensified, she agreed to let me take her to the hospital 25 miles away.

"Pray, Mom," she yelled as we took off. "Honey, the pains are getting real bad. Drive faster!" I put the pedal to the metal. A bolt of lightning crashed into the ground ahead of us. Carla huffed and puffed against the pains, then cried out, "The baby's almost here. Pray!"

And pray I did, like never before. Finally, we arrived at Collinsville. "Thank You, Jesus," I yelled as I pulled into the hospital parking lot.

After hurried preparations, two nurses wheeled Carla's gurney into the delivery room. Several minutes later our son was born.

"Well, he's a little early," said the doctor. "We'd better keep an eye on him for a few days, just for safety's sake."

Carla and I were so happy to have a son! Amazingly, he resembled my first son, Adam, red hair and all. "Hey, peanut," I whispered as I rocked Jesse Daniel in my arms. "I'm your Daddy. Welcome to the world." Then the nurse placed him back in his incubator.

I was thinking how great and merciful the Lord was for giving me a second chance to raise a son. But my euphoria was interrupted when the doctor said that Carla was hemorrhaging badly.

"Dick, this is looking serious," the doctor said. "I'm going to call for help."

Carla was turning yellow from her loss of blood. Her lips were white as death, a scene all too familiar from Sarah's birth. But something new was happening to me. I was full of faith and courage. Living under the Word had developed my faith in God's ability to triumph over Satan.

"Hey, Doc, no problem," I assured him. "Everything is going to be fine." I went to the lobby and made a few calls to Carla's parents and some friends to announce the baby's birth.

As soon as the doctor was able to free the placenta, the bleeding stopped. He said that Carla was going to be fine.

TWO MORE BRUSHES WITH SATAN

Two weeks before graduation, I was cleaning up the Git-n-Go store when two rough-looking guys came in. They were acting nervous.

"Hey, guys, what's up?" I asked cheerfully.

"Give me a pack of cigarettes," the big one ordered.

"Sure, no problem," I answered. I flipped a pack up onto the counter. "That'll be eighty cents, gentlemen," I smiled.

Recently, there had been a string of robberies in the Tulsa area, especially at convenience stores. In some cases the clerks had been shot in the head. Something told me I was about to be robbed.

"Give me all your money," the older man demanded.

The younger one guarding the door yelled, "Hurry up and open the safe."

"I can't do that, boys." I replied. "I don't have the combination."

The older guy came around the counter to check for himself. He hit the release button on the cash register and scowled at the $80 he found. He stuffed the bills into his coat pocket, then grabbed at me. Without even thinking, I broke his grip and threw him up against the soft drink machine.

Then I caught myself. *Bernal! This guy has a gun!*

For what seemed the longest time, we stared at each other. I found that I was smiling at him. I figured the Lord did not send me 1,800 miles to go through Bible boot camp, just to catch a bullet in the back of the head in a convenience store. Maybe I thought I could stare him down like Davy Crockett did that old bear!

Out of nowhere a set of headlights flashed through the front windows. The older man yanked his head and yelled, "Let's split!" The thieves scrambled for the door. Had God sent the white garbage truck that pulled up in front of the store? One relieved Bible school student breathed a deep sigh of thanks to His Maker.

Graduation night found us all down at the Tulsa Convention Center, decked out in our red caps and gowns. We were a splendid sight. Pastor Vince had flown in from Paradise to be with us for this great night of celebration. As the diplomas were being passed out, we waited patiently for our turn.

Just before our turn came, one of the Bible School professors took the microphone and said, "We have an emergency. Would Dick and Carla Bernal please call Franklin Memorial Hospital immediately?"

My intense fear caused a ringing noise in my ears as we made our way toward the foyer. Carla kept squeezing my hand

and saying, "Honey, honey," over and over, as if she were dazed. "It's okay, sweetheart, it will be fine," she repeated. "Whatever it is, it's going to be okay."

Richard Cardoza and Pastor Vince joined us in the lobby to offer support. *Man, I hate the devil for sure*, I told myself as I found the pay phone and got through to the doctor.

"Mr. Bernal, your baby sitter brought your son Jesse in here, and he is bleeding from every orifice. Can you come immediately?"

I told him it would take twenty minutes to get there. But as I hung up the phone and turned to Carla, I saw the strangest sight. She was dancing before the Lord, hands raised, a glow on her face, and praises coming from her lips.

"The Lord just spoke to me, honey," she said. "It's Jesse, isn't it? But he is going to be fine. The Lord just told me. Let's go back and get our diplomas."

"But I told the doctor we were coming right away. They'll save our diplomas. Let's go."

On the way to the hospital I recalled the vision the Lord had given me a month before. In the vision I was looking at the new bassinet when suddenly a large snake slithered into it. The serpent was about 20 feet long and looked quite hideous. When I came out of that vision I made intercessory prayer for Carla's health and for the well-being of our unborn child. God had forewarned me that problems were coming, yet assured me that victory would be ours.

At the hospital, the nurse directed us to the emergency room, where we were greeted by an apologetic attending physician.

"Hello, folks," said the doctor. "I am sorry to have alarmed you, but your son gave us quite a scare. Your friend Doug rushed Jesse in about an hour ago because he was bleeding from his rectum. Even his mouth and ears were seeping blood."

The doctor explained that they were having trouble stopping the bleeding, when all of a sudden, it just ceased! In fact, he said it had stopped about fifteen minutes before we arrived. Later we found out that at that very moment the entire graduating class had prayed for Jesse's recovery.

Jesse was transferred to a larger hospital in Tulsa for observation. They ran some tests in an attempt to locate the source of his problem. But nothing was found. Carla shared with the doctor how God had totally healed our son.

"Well, I can't argue with that," he answered. "We can't find one thing wrong with him."

Jesse was released on a Monday, and we headed for home. California, here we come! On the way out of town we stopped by Richard and Corrine Cardoza's home to say a temporary good-bye. They were waiting for their baby to be born. Then they would come to Paradise to be with us and with Pastor Vince.

Over the next two days of driving, I couldn't help but wonder what lay ahead for us. What was my calling? Pastor? No, too many headaches and heartbreaks. Evangelist? There were enough of them already. Teacher? I liked dissecting scriptures and explaining them to people.

Yeah, God willing, I could become a Bible teacher.

And God has appointed these in the church:
first apostles, second prophets, third teachers.
—1 Corinthians 12:28

Dick Bernal

CHAPTER 17

God's Will, Not Mine

Our first Sunday home, Pastor Vince asked me to share with the little congregation about the year in Oklahoma. Surprisingly, speaking from the pulpit felt natural. Vince took up an offering for us and peoples' generosity was heartwarming. That offering was just what we needed to buy groceries and get through the first week.

While Pastor Vince wanted me to work with him, the church was actually too small to support two ministers. So, Bible school diploma and all, I called my old construction company and went back to laying iron. Any spare time was spent helping around the church and being with my family. Pastor Vince knew I needed to share what I'd learned at school or burst. He let me lead the Sunday evening services.

Around October I began feeling antsy. *There is a world of people out there dying and going to hell,* I thought, *and here I am working on a bridge deck in Redding, California.*

One hot miserable day I arrived home from work and made my usual announcement, "Hey, everyone! Daddy's home."

Carla came down the hall. "Honey, guess who just called? Guess, honey!"

"Carla," I said, "I'm tired and thirsty, and in no mood for games."

"It's your sisters and Ed. They want to get saved." She explained that my brother-in-law Ed told her that he was suicidal.

"What did you tell him?" I asked.

"I said, 'Praise God, Ed!'"

"You said, 'Praise God'?" I asked incredulously.

"Yes," Carla replied, "I said 'Praise God, now Jesus can get hold of you.'"

Ed had answered, "Well, I don't know if I need Jesus, but I desperately need to talk to you and Dick."

My brother-in-law had always been one of my favorite people: successful, hard-working, and generous. Ed was a lot of fun and had a great sense of humor. But his drinking was getting the best of him. He and my sister Juanita were constantly at each other's throats. Carla told me they would be at our house at 11:00 p.m.

Ed and Juanita brought my other sister Judy with them that night. Ed was handsome in his expensive Western-style clothes. My sisters were dressed up in silk finery.

Ed drove us down to the local ice cream parlor in his brand new El Dorado Cadillac. As soon as we were seated, Carla jumped right in. "Ed, you need Jesus in your life."

"I need something," Ed replied.

We shared our experience of God's love and goodness for an hour. It was getting late, so we decided to call it a night. Back in our bedroom, Carla and I prayed that Christ would enter their hearts.

We all went to dinner at a local restaurant the next evening. I was looking at the menu when the Lord spoke to me: "Go home with Ed, son. This is going to take a while."

I said, "Ed, the Lord just spoke to me about you. He told me to go home with you after we finish eating and teach you His Word."

Ed stared at me with big eyes. "Dick, if you'll come home with me and teach me the Bible, I will pay you $500 a week."

"Done," I answered. There are some things in life you just know are from God.

Later as I sat in Ed's home I wondered where to start. The book of John? Maybe Matthew? Or why not at the beginning of the Bible? Yes, I'd start with Genesis and go from there.

After our first dinner at Ed and Juanita's home, we all gathered in the living room. I taught on creation. I could tell from their expressions that they were getting into it. Once in a while one of them would ask a question, which led to more questions. We stayed up for hours, night after night. Yet none of them were willing to commit to God with a prayer of repentance and salvation. So I just kept plugging along.

Then Lisa, my teenage niece, came down with a bad case of influenza. Juanita shared her concern about Lisa with Carla, who had been looking for a chance to demonstrate God's power to this family.

"Come on, everyone," she ordered. My brave little soldier for Christ marched us into Lisa's bedroom. With authority in her voice, she commanded the spirit of infirmity to leave Lisa, and she did not mean maybe. Both of us laid hands on Lisa's burning brow and praised the Lord in our heavenly prayer languages. Within minutes Lisa's fever left her.

When Lisa sat up and said that she felt much better, Juanita and Judy looked at each other in wonderment. They became willing to receive Christ as their Savior right then, and we prayed for them with great joy.

Two sisters down, but one stubborn brother-in-law to go. Instead of Ed getting closer to God, he started drinking more heavily and acting belligerent.

One night when I was praying for Ed, the Lord said, "Son, you are in a wrestling match with a demonic influence over the life of your brother-in-law. Keep persisting."

On Sunday morning we were dressing for church, when Ed stomped into the kitchen, sporting a monster hangover. "Where's the 'blankety, blank' orange juice?" he barked, jerking open the refrigerator and knocking over milk cartons and bottles. When he found there was no orange juice, he slammed the door as hard as he could. Cursing one and all, he stormed back into the bedroom.

He looks so sad, I thought. *His countenance is very dark.* I could sense a spirit of death hovering around him. Without hesitation, I followed him into the bedroom. He was buried beneath a pile of blankets and pillows as if he was trying to escape life altogether. I pulled back the covers, crawled into bed beside him, and began to weep.

Putting my arm around my poor, miserable brother-in-law, I said, "Ed, I'm not going to let you go to hell!"

Ed bolted out of bed as if he had been shot out of a cannon. "You're right," he declared. "Let's go to church."

Amen, hallelujah, thank you, Jesus, I shouted silently.

After church, we all went to lunch at the Los Gatos Lodge. "Well, how did you like the service?" I asked the family.

"Ah, okay, I guess," Juanita answered for them. Then she said, "Why don't you start a church, Dick? We like the way you teach."

At Bible school we had heard horror stories from former pastors who were ostracized by boards of elders and deacons for even the most trivial of things. Carla and I had practically made a covenant with each other that pastoring was not for us. No way! Forget it!

LEAP OF FAITH

Just as I was about to tell my sister that her request was impossible, that familiar voice from the depths of my being whispered a command. "Listen to your sister. She is speaking for Me. It is My will for you to pastor right here, son."

I gulped down the remainder of my orange juice, and reminded the Lord that my wife, who was sitting beside me, would probably divorce me, or at least shoot me, if I said yes to pioneering a work in the San Jose area. *Now, Lord, you wouldn't want to be responsible for a broken home, would you?* I asked silently.

No answer. Boy, I hate it when He does that!

Bracing myself, I turned to Carla. "Honey, I think God wants us to, uh— start a church here."

"Yeah, I know. He told me the same thing."

A chill rippled up my spine. A church in San Jose pastored by an inarticulate ironworker who had been saved for only four years and was fresh out of Bible school seemed funny and scary at the same time. Yet what were we to do? The Lord was calling us.

One night we were driving through the Highway 680 pass, right before it dips down into the Silicon Valley. The night lights of the Bay Area shimmered before us, all the way from San Francisco to San Jose. Words from a gospel song floated out from our tape deck: "Tell them for Me, please, that I Love Them..." At the same moment, Carla and I received a shared vision of the letters "W-O-R-D" hovering like a giant rainbow over the entire peninsula. "Wow! We knew what we had to do.

Back at Ed's house I agreed to become pastor of the little congregation comprised of Ed and Juanita, and Judy.

"So where do we start, Pastor Dick?" exclaimed Juanita.

She had me stumped. The Bible School didn't have a course on starting a church, and if one had been offered, I wouldn't have taken it. "Well, let's see," I said, feeling embarrassed at my ignorance. "We need a building, some chairs, a pulpit, and well, you know, church things."

Before the week was out, our congregation had grown from three people to five. Ed's daughter, Kendra, and her friend "Harley Helen," a former biker's girlfriend, had joined our ranks. What a crew! Also, Ed's three sons had been coming around a lot lately, so I thought maybe we could double our new church, if they took the bait.

Ed owned a small vacant warehouse on the east side of town. It was just a bare shell, but we decided to go for it.

We broke the news to Pastor Vince up in Paradise, and he agreed to ordain me. His only sorrow was that we would no longer be part of Paradise Christian Center.

Richard and Corrine Cardoza's baby girl had been born in July back in Tulsa. They had since moved to California. When I told them of our plans, they got excited and volunteered to help. This was starting to sound like fun. Everyone was pulling together for the cause of Christ, Ed's boys building a platform and pulpit for the new church.

Ron Etheridge, an old friend of Ed's, ran an office supply and gave us a great deal on 100 folding chairs. Cost did not seem to be an object to Ed, who by now was so hooked on Jesus that he wanted to do everything within his power to get this new church off the ground. To make sure of his salvation, Ed and I took a ride out into the country one afternoon and parked next to a creek bank.

"Ed," I said, "I want you to pray something with me, right now."

He nodded his head, and repeated this prayer after me:

"God, I have read in Your Word that I am a sinner who needs your grace and salvation. I accept Your Son Jesus as my Lord and Savior. I trust in Your promise that His blood was shed for me. Now please forgive my sins and give me an abundant new life. Send your Holy Spirit to help me know that this day I have been born into Your family forever. Thank you in Jesus' name. Amen."

Ed looked up at me with moist eyes. I saw a new serenity in his face. His broad smile told me that 40 years of running from God had come to an end.

OUR FIRST SERVICE

Saturday night, I was so excited I couldn't sleep. Carla and Harley Helen were in charge of praise and worship. They practiced to canned music nearly all night.

The third Sunday of November, 1980, saw 14 people show up for our first official church service—that included family members and Richard and Corrine, who had driven down from northern California.

Eighty-six empty chairs looked a little foolish, but we were pleased anyway. That first Sunday, I simply shared the vision Carla and I had received about bringing the Word of God to the Bay area. I explained that if the Holy Spirit was truly behind our vision, the church would prosper and grow. I gave an altar call for salvation, rededication, and for baptism in the Holy Spirit. To my amazement, four people came forward!

I was so caught up in the blessings of the Lord that I forgot to take an offering. Juanita began waving her checkbook back and forth to remind me. Our first offering was $125, and we were thrilled.

On Monday, a city official paid us a visit. He told us that the zoning of this industrial park did not allow for a church, so we could no longer meet there.

Well, Bernal, welcome to the wonderful world of pastoring, I told myself. It had not been 24 hours since our first service, and the city already had shut us down. Now what? Well, I had a few days to find an alternate meeting place. Where should I look?

"How about a hotel?" asked Carla. "They have meeting rooms, don't they?"

Ed suggested the Hyatt Hotel down on North First, a place he used to hang out at, especially during "happy hour." The space would cost $125 for the day. *Boy, that's our whole offering*, I thought, but undauntedly pressed on. We put a small ad in the newspaper announcing a non-demoninational Charismatic church, featuring a hometown boy as pastor.

Sunday morning, we arrived early to set up. The family showed up all decked out in their Sunday best. But I felt very disappointed that six of the people from the prior week didn't show up, nor did I ever see them again.

The second Sunday my palms began to perspire as I saw our little meeting room fill up with 32 people. We were growing after all, but could I keep the attention of this ethnically diverse crowd? Some of the men were dressed in suits and ties. Had they come to test this rookie preacher's anointing?

However, I got an amen or two during my teaching on faith, and several of the couples stuck around to get acquainted after the service. That Sunday morning group formed the nucleus and the future of our church. All but one couple are still with us today. Most are involved in leadership.

I wondered if God was honoring my spontaneous obedience despite my ignorance about pastoring?

Trust in the LORD with all your heart,
And lean not on your own understanding;
In all your ways acknowledge Him,
And He shall direct your paths.
—Proverbs 3:5-6

CHAPTER 18

Growing Pains

Our little church kept meeting at the Hyatt until February of 1981, when it became increasingly difficult to guarantee a room every Sunday. A couple of times we had to move to a different hotel, and that created confusion as folks tried to find us. We felt it was time to find a more permanent location. Also, the need to have more than just Sunday morning service was evident. These people had an insatiable appetite for the Word of God.

Our search led us to a small, antiquated library called Briner Hall, in the little town of Campbell, a suburb of San Jose. The owner of the building used it for weddings and different types of meetings. He liked the idea of using Briner Hall for church services. He let us have the building on Wednesday nights and all day Sunday for $700 a month. Even though that was a lot of money, we believed that God would provide.

With 80 chairs on the hardwood floors, the place looked more like a church. A massive fireplace and an ornate ceiling added appeal. We began holding church at Briner Hall with our congregation of about 50 people. As more were added to our flock, Richard Cardoza decided we needed to organize a ministry of helps.

On the way to church for our first Easter service, Carla and I drove by Cathedral of Faith, one of the larger churches in the Bay Area. It is pastored by my dear friend, Kenny Foreman. We could see the hundreds of cars piling into the parking lot. The church was well known for its excellent Easter drama presentation.

I encouraged myself with words of faith. *You know, Bernal, some day you also are going to have a great work that is going to impact the whole Bay Area. Pastor Foreman has been at it for nearly 20 years, so just be patient. As the Lord has blessed him, He surely will bless you.*

We pulled into our parking lot with its six stalls. When I walked into Briner Hall, I found that 120 people had shown up for our Easter service! I taught the Word with all my heart. At the altar call ten new converts came up and gave their hearts to Jesus.

After the service, a couple of well-dressed young men approached me. They introduced themselves as Robert and Lynn, and said they were in the computer industry. Actually, they were investors in one of the newly started computer companies of Silicon Valley.

Robert and Lynn said they liked what they saw and heard in our services. They asked if they could help us financially. Richard and I made an appointment to have lunch with them the next week. At that meeting they expressed how they both felt sent by the Lord to help our fledgling church. These two men gave us the financial boost we needed.

It didn't take long to realize that Briner Hall could only be a temporary stopping place. There was very little parking, no air conditioning or heating, and a fire station was across the street. Sometimes I listen to one of the old tapes from the Briner Hall days, and the sound of the sirens is very distinct. When a fire broke out somewhere, we would have to stop the service and let the trucks clear the station before we started up again. We used to laugh and blame the devil that every time I had a good message, a fire would break out.

And we needed something with facilities for children as

more families were beginning to attend. Visiting a YMCA building near Cupertino on the west side of town, we found facilities
that suited us perfectly.

"How many people does it hold?" I asked the person in charge.
"Oh, you can get about 300 people in the main room," he said.
Three hundred people! I thought. *Are there that many people
in the Bay Area who would want to come and hear me teach? Well,
we'll just have to wait and see.*

We agreed to $2,000 a month to have the premises from
Friday noon through Sunday night. That first Sunday, September
6, 1981, about 90 people came. I felt astounded by the wide range
of ages, ethnic groups, and economic backgrounds. Infants to
eighty-year-olds. African-American, Hispanic, Asian, and Anglo.
Millionaires and street people. The Lord was calling them one and
all. I remembered reading how during the first Pentecostal outpouring of the twentieth century at the Azusa Street revival in Los
Angeles, one of the most remarkable fruits of the Holy Spirit was a
lack of racial prejudice. Now almost 80 years later the same thing
was happening before my eyes.

DON'T BEAT THE SHEEP

Looking back over the first full year of pastoring, it amazes
me that the foolish things I attempted didn't sink the whole ship. I
really panicked during the first summer of slumped attendance,
even though this phenomenon plagues most churches. Richard and
I had been going out on Saturdays witnessing and inviting people
to our new church. Dear Lord, we met every conceivable type:
burned out druggies, flipped out Vietnam vets, fast-living bikers,
lonely housewives, and friendly senior citizens.

I had just read a book on soul winning, and it set me on fire.
Carla and I would go to shopping centers between Sunday services, pass out tracts, and invite folks to the evening service, which
usually averaged about ten people. I was determined to see the
church grow.

One Sunday in July, I decided to straighten out the congregation. "Either you can go out into the highways and byways with me to witness, or you can find another church," I told them. I felt righteous as I lambasted the crowd of 75 for their apparent lack of concern for the lost. I shouted, whooped, and hollered about the wages of slothfulness. I told them to show up next Saturday at church for their neighborhood witnessing assignments.

On Saturday, I drove up fully expecting an army of zealots. Instead, there was Richard, a young man named Scott, a young girl, and yours truly. Then I really got indignant. "If they thought last Sunday was scathing, just wait until tomorrow," I threatened. "I'm going to pin their ears back for good. Just wait and see."

The next morning I drove to church feeling like a fiery prophet sent by God. I pulled into a near empty parking lot. "Where are all the cars?" I asked Carla.

"You probably scared them off last week, honey," she gently replied.

"What? No way! They needed a little shaking up. They'll be here—won't they?"

At 10:00 a.m., Bill hit a few chords on his guitar and began leading the people in praise and worship. I counted...26, 27, 28 in attendance. I was still counting heads when I should have been worshipping God. At 10:30, the announcements were read from the church bulletin. No one else showed up. Carla's words rang in my ears.

That summer setback cost us over half the congregation. Instead of beating the sheep again, I changed my message to one more suitable for new babes in Christ. I worked on tempering my assertiveness with patience and love.

Not everyone is a Philip or a Paul. Many never will be. I prayed for the Holy Spirit to help me become more accepting of people, as God is.

> *But the fruit of the Spirit is love, joy,*
> *peace, longsuffering, kindness,*
> *goodness, faithfulness,*
> *gentleness, self-control.*
> *—Galatians 5:22-23*

CHAPTER 19

Dumb Decision

Richard and Corrine felt that God was leading them back to northern California to pioneer a church. We prayed for God to bless them, but I really felt the loss of my associate and confidant.

By now I was on full salary, relieving my brother-in-law of his commitment of $500 a week. We still had fewer than 100 members. My two young computer entrepreneurs told me that money was no object. They encouraged me to hire a new assistant.

About that time, one of my members introduced me to a young preacher who had just left a small church across town. Apparently he and the senior pastor had come into conflict over financial matters.

The out-of-work pastor was introduced to me Sunday morning. That night he and his wife returned for the evening worship service, and joined us for coffee afterwards. I took a liking to him and asked if he would like to work with me. I even dangled a salary and a title in front of him. He said he would discuss it with his wife and get back to me in the morning.

On the way home, Carla was real quiet. About a mile or two from home, she said, "Honey, why did you offer that man a job? We don't know a thing about him—his background, his doctrine, or anything."

"Oh, Carla, relax! He's okay," I reassured her. "I like him and I like his wife."

"That's not the point, dear," she retorted. "I like him too, but is he right for our church? Will he flow with our vision? You wouldn't marry someone after a first date, would you?"

"Carla, stop being so paranoid. This is different."

"Did you pray about it?" she asked.

I really hate it when she does that!

"Give me a break!" I complained. "I'm not totally helpless. God probably gets tired of me always bugging him with questions. I'm a big boy with a good head on my shoulders. Trust me, dear."

However, after a few months of trying to make our association work out, I could see that I had made a big mistake. The chemistry between us was all wrong. Our different personalities made it impossible to pull together as a team. A couple of years later this associate took several of our congregation to start his own church across town. But his church folded in six months because of his antagonistic pulpit style. This underscored to me that a pastor's personality plays an important role in the spiritual health of his ministry.

I also learned that a pastor who does not diligently seek the Lord before hiring key staff people must bear the pain when things backfire. Successful pastors have shared with me this important truth—your staff will make or break the church.

Pray without ceasing.
—1 Thessalonians 5:17

CHAPTER 20

Passage to India

By Christmas of 1981 our church had leveled off at about 120 people attending the Sunday morning services. I thanked God for the progress we had made, but wondered if the church had peaked out.

But my bigger question was why couldn't we keep growing? Why not become a church of two hundred or even two thousand? If God was willing—and the fact that He gave His only Son for our salvation shows unlimited willingness—then how might we expand our horizons in the kingdom of God?

The Bernal family had been one of the pioneering Spanish families back in the early 1800s. They were a tough, durable lot, forging a life out of a wilderness in the name of God and king. I burned with desire to impact the land of my forefathers. I figured if my Roman Catholic ancestors had the courage to press on, their Protestant Charismatic descendent could do no less.

NEW MARCHING ORDERS

I developed an insatiable interest in the dynamics of church growth. Why did some churches teem with excitement and run out of room for all the people, while other nearby churches got stuck on plateaus or downright deteriorated?

I started reading every book and article I could get my hands on about church growth. I would attend any minister's seminar within driving distance. My old church back in Tulsa announced a conference for new pastors. I knew I had to be there. One of the young businessmen in my church offered to underwrite my trip. Maybe he knew we needed all the help we could get for our infant church.

One of the conference keynote speakers was Dr. Lester Sumrall, a seasoned veterans of overseas ministry.

Morning, noon, and night, I sat there receiving instruction, correction, and especially encouragement from all the speakers. Dr. Sumrall, who since has become one of my dearest friends, laid his hands upon me and prayed for the anointing of God to go through me. Boy did I feel a jolt!

As I was leaving an afternoon session, I overheard a group of preachers talking about going to India next February.

India! I thought. *Oh, God, can you work this out? I've just got to go to India.*

I can't honestly say God told me in so many words to go to India, but I had a strong witness in my heart that I was supposed to go on this trip. So I walked up to the group, waited for the right moment, and piped up, "I'm interested in going to India too. How do I get to go?"

They told me to attend an afternnon meeting where different veterans of trips to India would talk about the proposed trip. I could hardly eat lunch, I was so excited to find out more.

That afternoon I heard different pastors expound on the "do's and don'ts" of the mission field to a small group of us. I trembled with anticipation.

They spoke about India's demons, idol worshippers, paganism, and snake charmers. *Oh, boy, this is going to be fun!*

I arrived home in San Jose late Saturday night and immediately shared with Carla my new passion about going to India.

"India!" Carla yelled in bewilderment. "Why do you want to go to India?"

"I just do, honey," I said. "I believe God would have me see a part of the world I have never seen. It would do me and our church good."

"Okay," answered my concerned wife. "But I'm not sure about all this."

The next morning I announced to my congregation, "Your pastor is going on a trip to India." Riding the tide of many "amens" and "hallelujahs," I figured it was a good time to announce my need for financial help. "And I need $2,000 to get me there and back—and cover living expenses."

There were only about 50 people there that morning. Many began standing and making pledges in various amounts. We started counting on the spot, until at $2,700, I yelled "Stop! That's enough. Gee, I didn't know you wanted to get rid of me that badly."

We all laughed and rejoiced together.

ALONG FOR THE RIDE

I met the rest of the team in New York at Kennedy Airport. Within a couple of hours, we were on our way across the ocean, with layovers in Paris, Kuwait, and other places too difficult to pronounce.

We finally landed in Bombay. I was so keyed up and full of French coffee that sleep was impossible. I had heard of culture shock and been told about India, but was not prepared for the sights, sounds, and smells of a Third World country. Aromas from exotic cooking spices, and stench from animal dung and open sewers filled the air.

Beggars jammed the streets. The poverty was overwhelming. Every now and then I'd see a cow wandering aimlessly about. Even though I'd been warned about the conditions, I could still barely comprehend what I was seeing.

"My God!" I exclaimed to one of the pastors. "Right here on our planet people are living worse than our pets do back home! Human beings—people for whom Jesus died—are living like gutter rats."

Another pastor leaned over and whispered, "I wonder if this is the result of so many people worshipping demon idols?"

I clutched my Bible, thanking Jesus for America and for my Christian faith. I couldn't help but picture my own children in this environment, shuddering from the thought.

Later, we caught a propeller airplane to the city of Hyderabad, near the center of India. From there, a train called the Krishna Express took us on a seven-hour journey across this mysterious, yet captivating country. With all of its poverty, there is a raw, stark beauty about India.

I noticed how kind the people were—almost childlike. Peeking over the backs of their train seats at the foreigners from America, they'd burst into giggles when we would catch them staring. We reached our destination late Wednesday afternoon, a place called Guntur. A large group from the Lutheran Church and Bible School greeted us.

Guntur is the headquarters for the Lutheran Church in Central India. Their missionaries would host this week-long preaching and miracle crusade. The promotional literature around town actually guaranteed miracles, signs, and wonders. I asked if I might have an opportunity to teach on the Bible. They quickly informed me that we were not here to teach but to preach to the lost—the Hindus and Muslims in particular.

Preach? I thought with alarm. *I've never preached in my life. I'm a Bible teacher. Now I'm 13,000 miles from home with a suitcase full of teaching notes, and they want me to be a Billy Graham!*

As we checked into our run-down motel, I noticed the strange wallpaper. It had lizards on it. "Why would anyone want lizard wallpaper?" I asked my roommate. Then I noticed that the wallpaper was moving. Gross!

Our hosts assured us that this was the best lodging we could get. Reluctantly, I flopped down on my rock-hard bed. A short while later a knock woke me out of a deep sleep. I answered the door feeling like a zombie.

One of our hosts told me that a meeting was taking place right away. Attendance was mandatory. A meeting! The last thing I wanted to do was go to a meeting with a bunch of preachers.

At the meeting I learned to my utter dismay that I was to preach that night in a town 40 miles away, whose name I still cannot pronounce. Apparently, our hosts had set up satellite meetings in several surrounding villages to promote the big crusade that would start in a few days in Guntur. My missionary zeal rapidly waned. I suddenly craved a hug from my wife, a square meal, and my own bed back home. But I brushed off my travel worn clothes and dashed out the door.

ME, PREACH?

A fellow American from Minnesota, myself, and three Indian brothers stuffed ourselves into a tiny cab and ventured out into the Indian night. A quiet settled over us as if we were commandos headed into the danger zone. Small candle-lit shrines, no larger than walk-in closets, appeared about every mile along the road. People knelt worshipping graven images. The sight gave me the creeps.

Demon worship, I told myself. *I wonder if any evil spirits will manifest tonight in our meeting?*

In a clipped British accent, one of the hosts turned and asked, "Reverend Dick, you will please preach for at least two hours, sir?"

Two hours? I had never preached two minutes. I smiled and nodded yes to my gracious host, while wincing at the thought. Then I turned to my American associate and told him it would please the Lord if he opened the program and shared what was on his heart for as long as he wanted.

He agreed. I hoped I had bought myself some time to get a message together. *Oh, God,* I pleaded, *help your poor undeserving servant get out of this mess—please!*

As we pulled into the grounds, I could see thousands of beautiful brown-skinned faces staring at us. Many began to stand as we made our way to the rustic makeshift platform. Music and singing had been underway for hours. I could make out the tune of the chorus *This Is the Day*.

After several introductions of everyone who was anyone— a custom you get used to on the mission field—Gayland, my preaching partner, was introduced to the crowd. I figured he was good for at least an hour. Hopefully, he might last an hour and a half. Certainly I could gather at least a few thoughts on something worth preaching about from my Bible.

But after a mere twenty minutes, I heard Gayland say, "And now, ladies and gentlemen, it gives me great pleasure to introduce to you one of America's great preachers, all the way from the San Francisco Bay area. Would you welcome Reverend Dick Bernal."

I thought, *God, if I shoot Brother Gayland, will I still make it to heaven?*

Struggling to my feet in a daze from lack of sleep and near terror, I whispered into the microphone: "Hello, everyone."

My little Indian interpreter followed suit—even to the whisper. I cleared my throat and took a deep breath. And so did he.

Is he an interpreter or a mimic? I wondered. *Boy, these guys are really trained.*

I began by sharing my lifelong desire to visit India, but had no clue where to proceed from there. Then out of nowhere came an inner prompting to share the story of Elijah, the prophet of God, and his encounter with Ahab and the prophets of Baal on Mount Carmel. I flipped the pages of my Bible to 1 Kings 18.

As I found the text, a strange sensation came over me. I felt as if an invisible person was pouring warm oil over my head. The sensation eased down through my body, transforming my fatigue and fear into a wonderfully exhilarating feeling of confidence. To my astonishment, I began to preach!

Hear me, O LORD, hear me,
that this people may know that You are the LORD God,
and that You have turned their hearts back to You again...
Now when all the people saw it, they fell on their faces;
and they said, The LORD, He is God!
The LORD, He is God!
—1 Kings 18:37,39

CHAPTER 21

The Holy Spirit in Action

Within moments I was prancing around the platform, shouting and challenging all the demons of that city to come for a shootout. We would prove that night whose God was the true and everlasting God. I felt like Elijah himself. An hour rushed by, and I was just getting warmed up. Sweat dripped off me, yet I was loving every minute. *I hope they are taping this*, I thought. *My home church will never believe this!*

Before I knew it another hour had zoomed by.

"Let's pray for the sick," yelled Gayland. "Especially those with respiratory problems. The Lord has given me a word for them."

"Sure," I said. "Let's do it."

I gave the invitation for people to come forward and receive Christ. I said that we would also lay hands on them for divine healing. But I was totally caught off guard when the enormous crowd bolted like a stampeded herd toward the platform. I had been preaching directly in front of the platform and the ministers had to reach down and rescue me from being crushed. It took nearly fifteen minutes to establish order out of the chaos.

We finally got the people to form two long prayer lines. I

looked down at my watch. It was nearly midnight. "Man, I'm pooped," I told Gayland. "Look at all these people. We're going to be here until dawn."

I was relieved to see no stretcher cases, leprosy, or deformities in my prayer line. In fact, they all looked fairly normal. Most of the people were young ladies with bright red dots on their foreheads.

"God," I prayed, "I have been bragging on you for two hours. I sure hope You don't disappoint these poor, needy people. Please bless them now."

I laid my hands on the first person, praying a blessing in Jesus' name and moved on to the next one. I quickly learned not to ask what was wrong, because people would tell me, alright. They'd tell me exactly what the doctor had said, and what their mothers, fathers, and grandparents had said. So instead I prayed for God to tailor His blessing to each need.

SIGNS AND WONDERS

I laid my hands on one young woman's head and began to bless her in the name of Jesus. She dropped to the ground as if shot, slithering like a snake and making gutteral noises. Her tongue darted in and out, while her eyes bulged out at me.

I froze. *What in the world is all this?*

No one around me did a thing. She slithered over toward Gayland, and I was very thankful that he was going to have to deal with her. I decided to continue praying and ignore the interruption. But then she was back, all curled up around my feet. She glared at me tauntingly.

"Demons, Reverend Dick! Demons," my Indian friends told me.

"I know that," I assured my hosts, trying to sound like an expert in demonology.

Three men picked her up and placed her in front of me. I recoiled at a demon literally looking out of her eyes at me. To cover up for my lack of training I just stared back at it. But as I attempted to pray for her, she broke free from the grip of the three men and began running for the road.

"Good riddance, lady," I murmured under my breath.

Instantly, the inner voice of the Lord commanded me, saying, "I didn't send you here to be mocked at, but to set people free. Go get her and deliver her in front of these people."

I had learned that when the Father speaks in that tone, obedience is mandatory. I sprinted after her, dodging between people. I caught up to this poor possessed soul and grabbed her arm. We both tumbled to the ground. She couldn't have weighed more than 90 pounds, yet she was imbued with incredible demonic strength. I tried to pin her down, but she threw me off like a rag doll. My skin crawled as it sunk in that I was literally wrestling a demon.

My three Indian minister friends caught up to us and began to help me. The four of us finally gained control of the girl. I used my thumbs to pry open her eyelids. An anointing from the Lord shot through me. I commanded the demon to leave in Jesus' name. It left her with a tearing sound. Her body went limp, and when she opened her eyes they looked peaceful.

We all stood up and regained our composure. When I realized that she could speak English, I led her in the sinner's prayer and had her denounce all her former idol worship. I instructed her to go home, destroy all the idols, and plead the blood of Jesus throughout her entire house.

We walked back to the two prayer lines and continued our work. About an hour later, several people led up a Hindu priest. An old man with long white hair, he wore a traditional orange robe and had his face painted like an Apache warrior—white and red stripes on his forehead and cheeks. His eyes were covered with milky-white cataracts. They told us he'd been blind for 8 years.

Gayland and I lay hands on his head and prayed in Christ's name for the restoration of his sight. The old man took one step forward and the white vanished from his eyes. He could see!

My mouth dropped open. *This stuff really works*, I thought. I watched as he started trembling under the power of the Holy Spirit. Tears poured down his cheeks as he turned his head this way and that, looking at everyone. A pastor told me later that the old man went to a little church in Narasarapit and walked around with his arms raised in praise all night along, saying, "Jesus, Jesus."

I continued praying in the healing line until the wee hours of the morning. I felt utterly exhausted, yet happy as could be. God gave me enough strength to last until all the people had gone home. That morning as sunlight filtered through the windows of my hotel room, I hit the bed with a thud, feeling awe at all I had experienced.

ACTS REVISITED

On the remaining nights of our crusade, God continued to show evidence of His signs and wonders. On the third night one of the people in the prayer line was an English-speaking father, dressed in a white shirt and dark slacks, who'd brought his seven-year-old son. He told me that his son was mute. The boy hadn't spoken in four years.

I prayed for the child, laying my hand on his forehead: "You fowl demon spirit—let him loose, in Jesus' name!" Then I knelt down to him. "Say hallelujah," I coached.

The little boy looked up at me. "Hallelujah," he whispered.

His father jumped, startled. So did I. Then I said to the boy, "Say Jesus."

The boy smiled and said, "Jesus!"

His father was so beside himself with joy that he started kissing me.

"Do you have idols in your home?" I asked the dad.

"Yes," he replied. "Many."

This didn't surprise me, since I had personally seen idols of gods like Vishnu and Kali in several of the homes I had visited. "Go destroy them at once," I declared. "Otherwise your child will become mute again. Now you serve the one true and living God." The simplicity of the Bible message struck me with new force: "For this purpose the Son of God was manifested, that he might destroy the works of the devil" (1 John 3:8).

By this time I began to feel an electrical power fill my body. I felt like there was nothing too hard for the Lord. A man weighing all of about 75 pounds, all crippled up, made his way towards me on a pair of handmade crutches. Suddenly, I heard the Lord command me to kick his crutches away, grab him by the arm, and start running. Not stopping to think, I kicked both crutches out from under this poor man and started running with him.

So here I am dragging him for about 30 yards and he's screaming the whole time. The Lord told me not to look at the man, but to just keep running. Finally the guy struggled up onto his legs and starting running with me like a Forrest Gump! We ran through crowd like track stars—a field of faith streaming over, around, and through us. People were cheering like crazy and crying out for the Lord.

When I got back to the platform, I became aware that the whole prayer team was so empowered by the Holy Spirit that thousands were accepting the invitation for Christ. People were crying or laughing or jumping for joy as the Holy Spirit witnessed within them that they, too, were now sons and daughters of the living God. I felt as if we were working alongside Peter and Paul in the book of Acts.

HOOKED ON INDIA

I returned to India ten years later for my own crusade in Guntur. I'd forgotten how desperate and childlike these people were. I felt like a real Christian walking among them, looking for ways to improve village life. Jubilee had given a missionary named Scott Norling several thousand dollars.

I took a drink from the first of several wells he had arranged to be dug with the money. In India a primary source of disease is contaminated water. By giving several villages wells dug deeply enough for pure water, Scott had positively impacted their lives.

During the trip the Lord spoke to me, saying, "You are called to this nation." I made a lifelong commitment to keep helping Indian villages with this life-giving project of providing wells, medical supplies, and the Word of God. To date our church has helped dig 50 wells.

But the 1995 crusade topped them all. That week the *Hindu Daily News* reported that we had ministered at "the largest gathering of humanity in the history of India to hear the gospel preached." Another reporter wrote, "Even Gandhi himself never drew such a crowd."

Our crusade lasted six nights, with 1.7 million people gathering to hear the Gospel message. More than 800,000 individuals received Christ as their Lord and Savior. Our latest crusade only cost 8.5 cents per conversion. Amazing!

Grant to Your servants that with all boldness they may speak Your word,
by stretching out Your hand to heal, and that signs and wonders may be done through the name of Your holy Servant Jesus.
—Acts 4:29

CHAPTER 22

A Bigger Vision

I came back from India in 1982 with a bad case of diarrhea, and fire from heaven burning in my soul. The first Sunday in my home church I felt catapulted into action, preaching and praying with unusual boldness. And there were results! The Holy Spirit moved upon people—one woman was healed of cervical cancer and many others were filled with the Spirit. In two weeks our attendance soared.

Soon our meeting room at the YMCA could barely contain the 250 adults. The children's rooms were packed. One warm Sunday in May, I looked out the sanctuary window and saw a traffic jam outside. *Is the Y sponsoring some other function?* I thought. I began my morning message, but was distracted by the head usher, who was looking around frantically.

"What's up, Scott?" I asked from the pulpit.

"Pastor," he said, "people are lined up down the hall, trying to get in."

I glanced out the window. Cars were circling the lot trying

to find a space to park. We stopped the service long enough to carry in chairs from an auxiliary room, squeezing in another 75 folks. I immediately announced that we would start having two services the next Sunday morning.

By the end of the summer of 1982, both services were totally filled. About 600 people, including children, were attending.

An opportunity came for me to start doing a radio program. I felt comfortable with radio, and pretty much preached up a storm, just the way I do in church. One Sunday morning two black sisters attended the Sunday service. Afterwards, one of these dear ladies, named Cora, came up to me and said, "I listened to you on the radio and thought for sure you were a black preacher. That's why I came this morning. Now I know you're a white boy, but I still like what you say. I think I'll keep coming back." Not only did she come back, but Cora and her sister Dorothy became Jubilee church mothers.

Over time, a larger influx of Afro-Americans came through the church doors. But their trust of a white preacher didn't come easy. I think Cora said it best. For three years she called me Dick or Mr. Bernal. Then a day came when she introduced me to one of her friends. My ears perked up when she said, "I'd like you to meet Pastor Dick." She had never called me her pastor before. And I had never taken issue about it, because a title of pastor has to be earned.

To keep up with the growth, I hired a full-time children's pastor from Oklahoma and a secretary. Our home phone was ringing off the hook with inquiries about this growing Charismatic church. The annual church income had steadily climbed to almost a half-million dollars. We kept our overhead low, which enabled us to bank $120,000.

It was obvious that the Y had outlived its usefulness. We needed a more permanent church home. Finding a new facility became my number-one priority, outside of prayer and study. Alan Vandermade and I scoured the whole South Bay area with little success. Places were either too big, too small, or too expensive. When we found places that fit our needs and pocketbook, the owners didn't want to do business with a church, especially one only two years old with no denominational backing.

Our two young investor friends, Robert and Lynn, came to the rescue. Robert and Lynn owned computer stock valued in excess of $20 million. Both men wanted to tithe to our church off their stock sales in the spring of 1983, when the company they had invested in would go public.

Alan and I spotted a vacant warehouse with 40,000 square feet we could use as a new sanctuary. The place would seat about 1,200 people. The asking price was $3.8 million for the building and the land.

Once the corporation's representative saw that we were serious and able to handle the transaction, a deal was struck. We occupied the building in March, 1983, on a lease option at $40,000 per month. We were counting on the tithe from Robert and Lynn's stocks in early summer to bring close to $2.5 million. Then we could get the monthly payments down to a reasonable level.

Everyone was all excited about our new and larger church home. Our first Sunday found 750 people in attendance with several visiting families. Kenny and Shirley Foreman, our dear friends and pastors of Cathedral of Faith in San Jose, congratulated us by sending over a beautiful floral arrangement.

Rarely a service went by where five or ten people did not come forward to find Jesus or to rededicate their lives. That first Sunday more than 30 people responded to the invitation. The next Sunday was Easter, and I had a lulu of a service ready that I had been working on for weeks.

"I wonder how many people are here," I whispered to Carla during the pulpit announcements. Afterwards I found out that there were more than 1000 people in attendance. Imagine that! More than 50 came to the altar to get right with God after the Easter morning sermon. The ushers proudly announced that the morning tithes and offerings brought more than $14,000.

What was all that silly talk about the hardships of pastoring? I asked myself. *Here I am with a new building, $2.5 million only weeks away, a church growing at a rate of two hundred people a* month, and invitations coming in from various places to speak.

Naturally, I spoke too soon.

FINANCIAL DISASTER

By midsummer the stock had still not gone public. Lynn dropped by my office one afternoon looking pale and nervous. He told me that the computer company had just filed for Chapter 11 bankruptcy. Not only were Lynn and Robert out several million dollars, but Pastor Dick was left holding a building that he and his church could not afford.

How do I tell the congregation? I thought.

I could just hear the devil gloating: "Well, big shot, maybe you can write a book on church death in one easy lesson. You're done, Bernal. It's over. Finished. I've got you now, boy. These people are going to abandon you and this church as soon as word gets out about how their pastor brought them to financial ruin."

I became so depressed. I refused to go to the office and would lie on the couch at home feeling sorry for myself. Even thoughts of suicide nipped my heels like rabid dogs.

My optimistic wife tried her best to cheer me up. "Oh, honey, God is our source, not some computer company."

Somehow, I was not in the mood for a Holy Spirit rally, even though I knew deep down in my heart that she was right. Against my wishes, she called an old friend from Tulsa.

It turned out that his church in Tulsa was also in a financial crunch, so we had common ground. After a couple of hours of ministry over the phone, I was able to say to him, "Yeah, you're right. No big deal. If God is in this work, it will all come out in the wash. If not, then let it die." I'm grateful for friends to whom I can turn in times of need.

The next day, I left home encouraged but realistic. *We've got a major challenge, Lord, but You're at the wheel, and I'll keep driving as long as You give me the go-ahead.*

When I got to my office, I discovered that Robert was waiting for me. For a man who had just lost several million dollars, he looked relaxed and confident. He told me he would borrow $100,000 to help us offset our negative cash flow. He virtually was wiped out, yet he managed to muster up funds for his church. I am happy to report that today Robert is doing just fine, as the Lord honored his sacrifice. And his generous offering gave us what the church needed to weather the storm.

I know how Peter felt when he was sinking under the waves and crying out for the Lord to keep him from drowning. Yet the real message of the Peter experience is that Jesus can turn a stunning setback into a glorious triumph for the kingdom of God. Glory to God!

> *But immediately Jesus spoke to them, saying, Be of good cheer! It is I; do not be afraid. And Peter answered Him and said, Lord, if it is You, command me to come to You on the water. So He said, Come.*
>
> *And when Peter had come down out of the boat, he walked on the water to go to Jesus. But when he saw that the wind was boisterous, he was afraid; and beginning to sink he cried out, saying, Lord, save me!*
>
> *And immediately Jesus stretched out His hand and caught him*
> *—Matthew 14:27-31*

Dick Bernal

CHAPTER 23

Facing My Limitations

1984 was one of those peak years. A new inflow of people began pouring through our doors, and most of them were staying put. As our church grew, I thought I was supposed to jump every time a member hollered. I ran from house to house listening to all the complaints and trying my best to put out all the fires. I figured counseling was a mandatory role of the senior pastor, so I opened my door to one and all.

One day I woke up to the fact that I am not a very good counselor. I enjoy praying, fellowshipping, and teaching the saints. But counseling definitely is not one of my strong points. So I appointed a counseling pastor. I was learning to accept my weaknesses, while concentrating more on my true strengths. I figured that if the apostles could admit their earthly limitations, so could I.

DREAM COME TRUE

By the end of 1984, we had around 1500 members. The income that year was $1.3 million. My dear colleague Richard

Cardoza had returned to shepherd the 150 students enrolled in our new Bible College. And the new day care center and K-3 Christian school were filling up rapidly.

Our praise and worship was boisterous and full of life. Carla said that my teaching and preaching skills were maturing. Jeff Hilbert, a young Bible School graduate, was doing innovative things with our children's programs.

The tenure in our warehouse was coming to an end, and we had seven months to relocate. Once again, Richard and I began feverishly combing the area for a facility. One day while driving into an area on the outskirts of town, we passed a handsome building with a red Spanish tiles on the roof.

My heart caught as I recalled the dream the Lord had given me just before going to Bible School. In that dream I was preaching to a huge crowd in a building in San Jose—a building with a red-tiled roof just like this one.

We struck a deal for the 54,000 square foot building. The monthly payment would be $50,000—a high price. But it was time to take another leap of faith.

> *And believers were increasingly added to the Lord,*
> *multitudes of both men and women.*
> *—Acts 5:14*

CHAPTER 24

Time of Testing

In early 1985 the American computer industry was hit hard when Japan practically took over the semi-conductor business. My phone was ringing off the hook with prayer requests from families who were losing their jobs and homes. Many people moved to Oregon or Montana to make a new start.

One spin-off was that the church's income leveled off—not a good sign in light of our recent move to the new 2,000 seat sanctuary! My only consolation was remembering how mini-revivals had rallied the people's spirits in the wake of previous moves.

I was hyped-up with enthusiasm. *Here we are in our new modern building. It won't be long before we fill this place us and have to expand to two services.*

But the surge did not come. In fact, we dropped slightly in attendance. The offerings remained under par. *What is going on here?* I wondered.

Some people said that it was because we had moved out to the boonies, that we were too far away from the population center of San Jose. Others felt the church had finally arrived, and we didn't need any more growth. But as we turned the corner on 1986, I felt increasingly frustrated.

"Lord, are you through with me here?" I asked. "Have I taken this church as far as I can? Should I turn it over to another?" There was no answer.

One morning from the pulpit, I let my feelings all hang out and shared my perplexity. People thought that meant I was leaving, so some of them up and left that very week. Friends began calling from around the country, asking if I was resigning.

Great, this is just great, Bernal. Your stupid little pity party is about to explode in your face. You had better rally the troops quickly, and get back on track, I exhorted myself.

It took some time, but I finally convinced the church that I was staying at the helm no matter what.

VISIT TO PRAYER MOUNTAIN

About this time one of our members, Sophia Choi, a precious little Korean lady, told me that a very special person wanted to meet me. Dr. David Yonggi Cho's mother-in-law was in town, and Sophia had told her about me. "Hallelujah Momma," as she is lovingly called, was delightful. With Sophia interpreting, we had a marvelous time of fellowship. I invited her to speak at our church, and she in turn invited me to speak at Prayer Mountain, Seoul, Korea.

Wow, the famous Prayer Mountain of Dr. Cho's that we've all heard about, I thought excitedly.

In May of 1986, 22 of us left for Seoul, a trip destined to change my life and the focus of the church. "Hallelujah Momma" kept us hopping while we were in Korea. She had me preaching all over town. My dear friend, Dennis Kim, a successful lawyer from Santa Clara, did the interpreting.

My first visit to Prayer Mountain shook me up. Driving up a winding road to the top, I saw a monumental auditorium built of concrete and wood. The chapel holds 15,000 people. Run by Pastor Cho's church, Prayer Mountain is completely self-sufficient. They grow their own rice and vegetables, and keep chickens and cows.

Prayer Mountain is used as a site for pilgrimages. The prior year 1.2 million people had visited the mountain—some fasting and seeking the Lord for weeks at a time. There are hundreds of prayer grottos scattered throughout the area—small concrete bunkers in which a single person can kneel on a straw mat.

The compound sits just 8 miles from the DMZ zone that separates North from South Korea. Dr. Cho's congregation see themselves as prayer warriors, who pray daily for the reunification of Korea. They rebuke the powers of darkness in active spiritual warfare. I was impressed by the economic growth of South Korea and the great spiritual vitality of the people.

That Sunday I was introduced to Dr. Cho, the pastor of the world's largest church, with 700,000 members. As a teenager, Pastor Cho was converted from Buddhism on his death bed. He has faithfully followed the Lord's direction for church building all these years. I was impressed by his transparency and openness, and felt highly honored to have met a real saint of God.

WORSHIP AND PRAISE

As soon as we returned home, I reemphasized the basics of successful Christian living. I taught from the Word, instituted daily prayer times with fasting, encouraged members to witness, and sought to love and worship God in our services. The Lord guided me to focus on faith and covenant living, righteousness and authority in Jesus' name, and other basic doctrinal truths. Getting back to the basic fundamentals of our Christian faith did wonders for our church. Attendance and offerings began to increase as the Lord blessed our efforts.

Along about this time we made a key change in our approach to worship. Carla and I felt like we had fallen into a predictable routine of singing the same old songs Sunday after Sunday. There was nothing wrong with this, except that it seemed to be putting people to sleep. I wanted to wake everyone up!

A friend told me of a gospel singer named Ron Kenoly who was looking for a position. "He sounds just like Lou Rawls," said the friend.

"Lou Rawls," Carla blurted out. "I love Lou Rawls."

We arranged for Ron to come to a service and sing a couple of songs. Ron took the mike and opened his mouth. It didn't take Carla ten seconds to make up her mind. "Hire him tonight," she said, with that look of assurance.

"Hey, I thought I was the impetuous one," I said in exasperation. "Okay, sweetheart, if you think so, so be it." Now, friends, that was one of our better decisions over the last 15 years of ministry. As you may have guessed by now, my wife's spiritual intuition proves to be right on the money nine times out of ten. Though I get annoyed about how right she can be, I really respect her guidance when the Lord moves on her.

Ron still ministers faithfully on our staff, but he has also become a globally recognized and sought after worship leader. Some call him the Billy Graham of praise and worship. His CD's, videos, and cassettes sell by the millions.

Recently someone asked me if I was jealous over Ron's astounding success. "Are you kidding?" I replied. "Ron's success is my success. It's Jubilee's success. We all benefit from what God does through Ron and his gift."

And Ron mobilized a mighty army of skilled musicians and singers that filled Jubilee Christian Center with praise of the Lord Jesus Christ as never before. Not only did some people return to our church, but hundreds more started coming for the first time, and joined our family.

I learned a great lesson in 1986. Thank God for new buildings, but in the end these structures are merely brick and mortar. The heart beat of a growing church is doing the Father's will, welcoming the Holy Spirit, and loving Jesus as He loves us.

And when he had consulted with the people,
he appointed those who should sing to the LORD,
and who should praise the beauty of holiness,
as they went out before the army and were saying:
Praise the LORD, For His mercy endures forever.
—2 Chronicles 20:21

Dick Bernal

CHAPTER 25

Lucifer Comes to Church

For the sake of anonymity, I'll call the two men I refer to in this chapter as Darren and Pedro. At a time when I was looking for an assistant, Darren appeared, and his credentials were impeccable. He had worked for over six years for a national ministry, and had been ordained with a major Pentecostal denomination. Darren was on a first name basis with many leaders in the Charismatic movement. I thought I had signed up a home-run hitter to our pastoral team. But just as Lucifer is said to pose as an angel of light, so there can be those in the church who harbor dark intentions.

Darren had been a member of Jubilee since 1985. I was able to watch him up close and first hand. To all appearances, he was an effective leader who inspired those around him and worked tirelessly for the kingdom of God. What I didn't know was that the man was a pedophile. He began preying on young men in our church.

The shocking phone call came at around one in the morning. Sleepily, I fumbled for the receiver. *Who in the world would call me at this hour, especially on a Sunday night?* The familiar voice was that of my friend, Ed Silvoso.

"Dick, I have some disturbing news that can't wait."

"What is it, Ed," I replied, sitting up and waking Carla.

He told me that Darren and Pedro were being accused of molesting a young boy in the church.

"What! You're joking."

"I'm afraid not, my friend."

Ed gave me the details of how he got wind of this mess. Darren was my administrative assistant and Pedro was our Junior High leader. A mother was working on a hunch that her son, who had struggled with homosexuality before attending Jubilee, was involved with both Darren and Pedro.

The next morning, I went to the office and summoned Darren and Pedro to my office. I wanted them to hear the accusation from me before they heard it from anyone else. Darren exploded into rage and vigorously denied the charges. He pounded on my desk, proclaiming his righteous life. Pedro sat quietly, looking nervous and guilty.

Darren's defense sounded so plausible that I hoped he was telling the truth. What I decided to do was to investigate the matter for myself.

That very day Carla and I talked with the young man's parents. They agreed that I could talk with their son. When he arrived home he looked totally abashed to see Carla and me in his living room.

"Hi, Pastor Dick, what are you doing here?"

"Son, we need to talk. Can we go somewhere private?"

"Sure, Pastor, let's go to my room."

I sat on his bed. He sat in a chair. "Son," I said, "Do you know why I'm here?"

"I think so," he replied sheepishly.

"If Jesus was sitting here with you, would you answer Him truthfully?"

He nodded.

Under my breath, I was still praying, *Lord, don't let this be true.*

"Have you and Darren or Pedro ever had sexual relations?"

He sat there for several moments staring at me, then lowered his head and spoke openly about the molestation.

I felt disgusted by what I heard, yet thanked him for his courage. I stood up to leave.

"Pastor," the young man said, "Darren and I are lovers. Please tell him I still love him. Will he be okay?"

Now the disgust practically overwhelmed me. I just shook my head, foreseeing the scandal that this would hit the church. As I entered the living room, Carla and the young man's parents looked at me anxiously.

"I'm sorry to say, but it's true," I whispered.

His mother broke into sobs. Carla grabbed her, trying to offer comfort. A familiar feeling from childhood wrapped its scaly arms around me. I felt ashamed. Why hadn't I seen through the sheepskin into Darren's wolfish heart. *This will be the end of Jubilee*, I feared.

Needless to say, I tossed and turned all night. On Monday morning I called Darren into my office. George Richardson, our comptroller at that time, sat in on the meeting. I had already briefed him.

Darren looked ashen. He knew judgment day had come. Somehow I felt so sorry for him. He and Pedro had put the whole church's future in jeopardy. But still he was a human being, a friend, and one sick man. I recounted what I'd been told by the young man. Darren just stared at the floor, not moving for over ten minutes. I could see a large vein pulsing on his balding head.

My God, Darren, how did you ever come to this? I thought.

Darren finally lifted up his head and stared at me blankly. "What do you want me to do, Pastor?"

"If this is all true, Darren, you must resign immediately. And let's get you some help."

He slowly nodded his head up and down, then got up, and staggered out of my office. "God Almighty," I said to George, "what now?"

The following Wednesday night Carla, Pastor Brian, and I

went to visit Darren at his home. I felt worse than being at a funeral. Darren admitted to some of the charges, telling us he felt he was in a pit with a monster. If he didn't involve himself in certain activities, he rationalized, the monster would devour him. Carla broke down and wept, holding Darren in her arms.

That was the last night Carla and I had any fellowship with Darren. As we left that night I knew the months ahead were going to be tough.

We immediately reported the story to the Child Protective Services, knowing that it was the right and lawful thing to do. No way around it. The future of Jubilee was at stake.

The police arrested Darren and Pedro. But when interrogated, both men sang a different tune. No longer repentant, they vehemently denied the charges. According to them, everyone was lying, including me. The story hit the news. All the local television reporters showed up licking their chops. The *San Jose Mercury News* did a big write-up. My phone rang off the hook. The international wire service picked up the scandal. Even Pastor Cho in South Korea read about it in a local Seoul newspaper. He called to offer me hope and support.

I broke the news to the church, doing the best I could to sound merciful, yet strong. I wanted to go bury my head in the sand.

BACK DOOR EXODUS

We lost a number of Jubilee families because of this incident. Some people blamed me for not having enough discernment. Others said that if I'd had more of a prayer life, this would never have happened. I had loaned one man a large amount of money to save his home. He vanished into thin air, but later said to one of our members, "How could I stay at Jubilee when my buddies at the country club were teasing me?"

What hurt the most was people I had married, visited in the hospital, and vacationed with, leaving the church. The wound was deeper than anyone will ever know. To help me through the ordeal, my secretary graciously shielded me from many angry letters which poured into my office.

For the next two years, Darren was in and out of jail facing the many charges that kept surfacing against him. Through it all he pointed the finger at me and Jubilee as the real culprits, denying his own culpability. But it didn't work. In April of 1995, Darren was sentenced to 19 years in prison.

Pedro, on the other hand, was remorseful and repentant. He pled guilty and cooperated with the District Attorney's office. I believe that with God's help, Pedro can lead a restored life after prison.

Beware of false prophets,
who come to you in sheep's clothing,
but inwardly they are ravenous wolves.
—Matthew 7:15

Dick Bernal

CHAPTER 26

God Is Good, Isn't He?

I can attest to the ups and downs in establishing the kingdom of God. But for every down there are abundantly more ups!

My greatest thrill, and one of those lifelong treasured moments, occurred in 1989. One Saturday Adam dropped by to visit his dad. This was not to be a casual time of catching up. His eyes were red and puffy. "You okay, son?" I asked.

"Dad, I've got to get right with God," my number one son exclaimed. I had led Adam to Christ when he was 12 years old. We had been fishing out at my favorite bass lake. In fact, Adam was my first convert.

But like many new converts, Adam faced numerous pressures from culture and peers that eventually undermined his faith. Carla and I agreed we wouldn't pressure him to attend church with us. We simply prayed for him, knowing that one day he would make the right choice.

Now, at 25 years of age, the Holy Spirit was moving on Adam in a most intriguing way. He and his girlfriend had been headed up to Lake Tahoe to drink and party, and God knows what else. But during the drive, his girlfriend began reading him one of my books. She read the part about how after a long life of self-will, I had finally surrendered everything to Jesus. Conviction fell on Adam. He turned the car around and headed home.

That Saturday morning we prayed together. I gave him a bear hug. Adam rededicated his life to Christ. Wow! There is no feeling like helping your own child find God!

Today Adam is our youth pastor, activities director, and a fine young man. Like his dad, he's hit a few speed bumps along life's highway, but being the resilient type, he hangs in there. The day I hired Adam to work for me Carla said to me, "Hey Pastor Dad, how's it feel to have both your red-headed sons under one roof?"

Recently, I had a commitment to give the devotional prayer at a Sunday lunch with the First Lady.

"I want you to take over the third Sunday morning service," I told Adam.

"What'll I say, Dad?" he asked, looking a little nervous.

"Just relax and talk from your heart," I coached. "God will do the rest."

Boy was I one proud father, leaving my son to fill the pulpit and preach his first sermon. God is good, isn't He!

As for me and my house, we will serve the LORD.
—Joshua 24:15

PART THREE:

WARFARE AND THE KINGDOM

For we do not wrestle against flesh and blood,

but against principalities, against powers,

against the rulers of the darkness of this age,

against spiritual hosts of wickedness in the heavenly places.

—Ephesians 6:12

Dick Bernal

CHAPTER 27

Take Your City for God

After writing a book called *Storming Hell's Brazen Gates,* I became known for my teaching on spiritual warfare. In the book I challenged Christians everywhere to give up their complacency and go to war against Satan and the powers of darkness. One of my favorite Scriptures tells how Jesus overcame the works of the devil. "For this purpose the Son of God was manifested, that He might destroy the works of the devil" (1John 3:8). So as Christ's disciples, we must press forward assertively to kick Satan out of our cities.

One of the most ingenious ways of defeating Satan is to offer people healthy spiritual alternatives that expose the devil's counterfeits. For instance, Jubilee Christian Center sponsors a night-club for local youth called Club J. The great atmosphere, music, and camaraderie draw kids away from Satan's turf.

Another idea we had was to put on a big prayer rally in downtown San Francisco on Halloween night. This was offered as a spiritual alternative to one of the raunchiest Halloween parties in America. Between 300,000 and 500,000 homosexuals, lesbians, witches and lookie loos gather in the Castro District to let it all hang out—and do they ever! Mardi Gras has nothing on this night.

In 1991 Pastor Larry Lea and I prayed about gathering 10,000 prayer warriors in the Civic Center Auditorium on Halloween night. People from our churches reacted enthusiastically. In fact, we raised nearly $100,000 for the event after our normal tithes and offerings. It was to be!

Larry and I weren't aware that the Castro District was just a few blocks from the Civic Center Auditorium. We certainly were not prepared for what was about to take place. The press picked up on the prayer meeting with headlines something like, "God's green berets invade San Francisco!" The article made us look like a bunch of right-winged political activists coming to curse gays, liberals, and the city itself. Nothing was farther from the truth. Our intention was to offer an alternative on Halloween night by inviting God's love and power into the city of San Francisco.

Then Dr. Eric J. Pryor got into the act. A Wiccan priest of the Temple of the New Earth, he was outraged after reading the article in the San Francisco Chronicle. Intending to put a curse on all involved in the prayer meeting, he called Jubilee Church. Mr. Pryor left a scathing curse on our church's answering system on October 29th.

By now the wire service had started a feeding frenzy. CNN, ABC, NBC, CBS, Current Affair, Inside Edition, and even a paper in France were calling my church office for interviews. Larry Lea was hiding out nursing a hernia and left most of the press to me.

To protest the prayer meeting, Eric busied himself organizing various pagan and homosexual groups, like Act Up and Queer Nation. He spoke on CNN, calling us witch-burners and bigots.

On the morning of my forty-sixth birthday, Larry and I made the front page of the *Wall Street Journal*. Later we appeared in *USA Today* and *Newsweek*. So here I am furiously fending off calls, reporters, cameras, wondering when Larry is going to show up and take a little heat off his ol' pal.

Eric's picture was in the *San Francisco Chronicle*. What a sight! A skinny, sickly looking young man with a shock of bleached blond hair, he wore a priest's collar with a pentagram hanging around his neck. His nose was pierced by a ruby. Just the kind of wierdo you pray your daughter doesn't bring home.

Carla felt sorry for him. "Oh, honey, he just needs Jesus like the rest of us." That night she put his picture on her stomach and prayed for hours. She wept over his soul, then petitioned the Lord to bless Eric and all of San Francisco in a mighty way.

Our friend Peter Wagner, a noted author and speaker, called Carla at home. He felt a great victory was about to be won and that one of Satan's generals would be saved. Now, Peter is fairly conservative about giving a prophetic word. So this word from him really bolstered our faith.

SHOWDOWN

A local CBS affiliate invited me to a morning talk show called, "People are Talking." They wanted me to explain our purpose for going to San Francisco. To my surprise, I was to be pitted against none other than Dr. Eric Pryor. As Carla and I were ushered into the green room for coffee and make-up, Mr. Pryor slipped in for the same.

"Hello, Eric, how are you today?" I asked, sticking out my hand.

Eric looked up sheepishly and put his hand in mine. Eric is not a big man. He looked as if he could use a good meal.

"Eric, after the show how about you and me having lunch at the Hilton where I'm staying? I'd like to explain to you our real purpose for this meeting."

"Sure, I'd be glad to."

The show came off like a real zoo, because the host kept trying to pit Eric and me against each other to see who would draw first blood. I didn't take the bait. Afterwards, Carla and I treated Eric and his girlfriend to coffee and nachos. I shared that our reason for the Christian get-together on Halloween was to pray in a positive way for San Francisco. Before long we were witnessing to Eric and Sondra about Jesus. I could see a visible change in his countenance as we talked.

I felt a liking for this young couple, and we all laughed together several times.

On an impulse that I now believe came from the Holy Spirit, I leaned over and asked Eric, "Would you like to be my special guest tonight at the meeting? You can sit with Carla and me and see for yourself what it's all about."

"Sure, Pastor Dick, I'll go," he responded.

We met him at 6:00 that evening. The three of us piled into Carla's car and made our way to the Civic Auditorium. I wasn't prepared for the sight of over 3000 hostile homosexuals shouting obscenities, hurling things, and being dangerously out of control. The police seemed overwhelmed. We parked and got out of the car. The crowd cheered when they saw Eric and booed when they saw me.

We pushed our way through the crowd and into the auditorium. Hundreds from our church shouted and waved to Pastor Dick and Carla, but looked stunned when they saw Eric at our side.

I overheard someone say, "Isn't this the guy who started all the problems? He cursed our pastor and our church."

One of Larry Lea's men came up to me and whispered, "What's Mr. Pryor doing here, Pastor?"

"It's okay," I assured him. "Eric is my guest tonight. He'll be fine."

I glanced around and counted almost 30 news reporters. Most were inching their way toward Eric and me. Larry preached magnificently that night. Eric seemed moved by the message, as we all were.

The crowd outside the prayer rally finally dispersed when the police threw a teargas bomb into the crowd. That's one Halloween I'll never forget!

The day after Halloween, Larry got together with Carla, Eric, and me. Larry gave Eric a Bible and challenged him to dig into the Scriptures and find out for himself who Jesus really is. Eric agreed and we all prayed.

Carla and I stayed in touch with Eric for the next three weeks. We gave him a standing invitation to visit Jubilee for a

Sunday morning service. One morning he came, and at the end of my message, he gave his heart to Christ.

For Thanksgiving dinner, 1990, our guest was Dr. Eric J. Pryor, former witch and priest of the New Earth Temple. I looked across the table at the born again soul, as Eric bowed his head in prayer for the meal. Dr. Peter Wagner had been right on with his prophetic word. One of Satan's former generals had become a Christian soldier.

The Spirit of the LORD is upon me,
Because He has anointed me to preach the gospel to the poor;
He has sent me to heal the brokenhearted,
To proclaim liberty to the captives...
To set at liberty those who are oppressed;
To proclaim the acceptable year of the LORD.
—Luke 4:18-19

CHAPTER 28

Reunion at The Stick

On Halloween of the following year, 20,000 Jesus fans gathered with Larry Lea and me at Candlestick Park. The stadium is home to the San Francisco 49ers and Giants, but with God's help it became a wonderful place for a spiritual holiday event. Eric Pryor sat on the platform with Carla and me, and Dr. Lea once again proclaimed that Jesus is Lord over the whole Bay Area.

However, when Diane Sawyer of Prime Time Live got wind off this, she put a different spin on it. She told her audience on national television that Larry and I had bribed Eric and faked his conversion to Christ. She also accused me of faking Eric's marriage to Sondra.

I called ABC in New York and spoke for 90 minutes with a Miss Sutherland, who was one of the producers of Prime Time Live. I explained every detail of Eric's conversion, and told her how he had been forced to move out of San Francisco because of death threats. In this vulnerable time of transition, Larry and I had helped Eric with $500 a month for an apartment near Jubilee, where he attended church regularly. Someone else had given Eric an old beat-up car to help out with transportation.

"Thank you Pastor, for enlightening us," said Miss Sutherland. But the show itself reflected no enlightenment. During the first 20 minutes Diane went after a preacher named W. V. Grant, Jr. I had barely heard of him, but I had to admit her story was very convincing. The next segment featured Larry Lea from Dallas, Texas, and also mentioned me. I couldn't believe what I saw. Lies, half-truths, and gross exaggerations made it look like Larry and I were a couple of flim-flam artists.

My blood hit the boiling point when Sawyer portrayed Eric living in an expensive condo on a golf course. She said I'd wined and dined him so that he would cooperate. The truth was that Carla and I coffee'd and nacho'd him as we'd shared about Christ.

Diane is good. She comes across sincere and believable, but so can Satan himself. I recognized in her cool vehemence that the world does hate Jesus and those who follow Him.

"Honey, she's lost and blind," Carla reminded me. "She thinks she's doing good. Just pray for her."

The next Sunday, Prime Time cameras were in my church. I had a little explaining to do to my congregation. The sheep were a little nervous. During my sermon time I answered every question raised by the telecast, and brought out the facts of Eric's conversion. The cameras rolled, but Diane never televised my rebuttal. I wonder why?

Did people leave the church over the Prime Time program? A few did, but not many. Actually, our congregation grew stronger through the ordeal. Thank God!

YOUR OWN BACKYARD

In the spring of 1992, America was stunned by what took place in Los Angeles. Late in the afternoon of April 29, south central Los Angeles erupted in rioting, looting, arson, and killing. The immediate cause of the outburst was a jury verdict rendered earlier that day. Four white policemen were found not guilty of assault in the beating of an African-American named Rodney King.

When the violence began, Los Angeles Mayor Tom Bradley imposed a curfew. Even so, the rioting and looting lasted three days. It was the worst urban disturbance in 20th century America. More than 54 people were killed. Over 5,000 buildings were destroyed or badly damaged. At least 4,000 people were injured and more than 12,000 arrested. Thousands of jobs had been lost and whole neighborhoods wiped out. The rioting got a head start on the police because the verdict was so unexpected, and the reaction so sudden.

Jubilee is full of African-Americans, Hispanics, and Koreans. Many had family members and friends in this part of Los Angeles. The Sunday following the 29th of April, I preached on the Good Samaritan. I must have heard my own sermon because I took $50,000 out of our general fund, leaving us with $4000.

I headed south in the company of my wife, Pastor Brian, who is African-American, and Dennis Kim, who is Korean. We were on a mission to bring love and assistance to a hurting city. I felt that the church ought to be the first ones involved in recovery. The congregation was totally behind us. We gave the money to a general recovery fund.

Later that day we went to the very spot where the riots broke out. Oh, for sure I had my oil with me. Brian led us in worship. Then Dennis, Carla and I asked Christ to forgive the sins, and cleanse both those who participated in the riots and those who lived in the area.

We asked the Father for a fresh outpouring of love from the Holy Spirit, for a spiritual unity to replace hate and hostility. We finished our prayer time and headed for the airport to return to San Jose. We knew we had done what we could.

When they pray toward this place and confess Your name,
and turn from their sin because You afflict them,
then hear in heaven, and forgive the sin of Your servants...
that You may teach them the good way in which they should
walk.
—1 Kings 8:35-36

CHAPTER 29

The Wall Of China

We are learning at Jubilee that the praise, worship, and spiritual warfare that happens in our city can spread around the globe.

Chinese evangelist Nora Lam and her whole family joined our church, and before long Carla and I had become good friends with them. Nora was always after me to go with her on a tour to China. One afternoon at church, little Dottie Bankus, our resident prophetess, came up to me and said, "Pastor, the Lord wants you to go to China soon."

I told the Lord I was not going unless He provided tickets for me, Carla, and the children. Plus, I needed to feel a witness in my spirit about such a trip. The very next Sunday a family told us they would pick up the tab for Carla and me, Jesse and Sarah, and would provide us with spending money to boot.

"All right, Lord," I shouted inside, "I get the message!"

We left San Francisco for Taiwan and mainland China. Our dear friends, Dr. James Pippin and his wife, Alene, were traveling with Nora. We also met Paul and Jan Crouch, who were very friendly. As soon as our group entered communist China, we could all sense the demonic spirit of oppression. I could not help but compare the spiritual exuberance of South Korea to fearful restrictiveness of Red China. Perhaps someday a great Pentecostal wave will wash over mainland China. Why not?

Eventually we reached Beijing. The oppressive atmosphere intensified in the capitol city that controls all of Red China. That morning, we gained an audience with the assistant ambassador from the United States to China. He told us of the great changes in China since President Nixon's visit in the early seventies. He said that the Bamboo Curtain had come down, and that the Chinese were open for exchanges with the Western world, that there was a desperate need for technology and innovative ideas.

The Underground Church in China is alive and flourishing, but it is in dire need of tools for evangelism. Nora introduced me to a Chinese pastor who spent 22 years in prison because of his faith. Two of his fingers had been cut off in an attempt to break his spirit. I will never forget that man's eyes, how peaceful and kind they were.

Bernal, are you made out of the stuff this man is? I asked myself silently, looking at all fingers and two thumbs on my hands.

"I'm glad my children are here to see all this, Lord," I whispered. "Thank You."

As we left the little church, Paul Crouch slipped the pastor a love offering and patted him on the back. I too, left some funds as a gift from Jubilee. As I handed him an envelop, I looked into the Chinese pastor's eyes again.

Oh, God, keep me sweet and humble, please, I prayed as we walked down the back stairs into the cool, Chinese night.

During our stay in Beijing, I periodically awakened from deep sleep, sensing a presence in the room—an evil sinister personality. One night I bolted up in bed and saw a shadowy apparition dart away. I woke up Carla and we began to pray out loud for Christ's blood to cover the room and the demons to depart.

The next day, we visited the Great Wall, a real monument of human endeavor. Matt Crouch—Paul and Jan's youngest son—had brought television equipment to capture the trip and show it back home on the network. As Paul, Nora, and Jan were being taped, sharing about their dreams and desires for China, they broke into intercessory prayer. Jan had a vision of a ruling prince swooping down at them. It was a hideous, evil-looking spirit, unhappy with our intrusion on its turf. Jan began shouting the name of Jesus and pointing her finger at the principality, and he vanished.

That day at lunch, Paul and I discussed how spiritual warfare involves the pulling down of strongholds over cities, even whole nations. We stated our agreement with Pastor Jack Hayford that cities—whether American or Chinese—need to be taken back from the enemy by the prayers of anointed Christians.

Back in the States, Paul invited Carla and I to host the TBN "Praise the Lord" program a number of times. We often ministered about spiritual warfare. I didn't realize it then, but we were foreshadowing a very bold venture into the heart of Communist darkness after the Tiananmen Square massacre, two years later.

TIANANMEN SQUARE

Can you picture this scene? On January 1, 1990, a little army of God's prayer warriors, clutching official papers, marched into the middle of Tiananmen Square. Suspicious government soldiers eyed us every step of the way. What had brought us there?

On June 3rd and 4th, 1989, the People's Liberation Army had brutally crushed pro-democracy supporters in Tiananmen Square, killing an estimated 3000-5000 people, injuring another 10,000, and arresting hundreds of students and workers. The violent suppression of the Tiananmen Square protest caused widespread international condemnation of the Chinese government.

Political strings had to be pulled before our little group was allowed out onto the square. Soldiers marching in cadence kept peering at us.

The square itself is enormous. It seemed to take forever to make our way to the center. I looked down at the tank tracks and bullet holes etched into the pavement—a silent memorial to the thousands who laid down their lives for freedom.

Ron Kenoly led us in praise and worship. Rachel Flores, one of my personal intercessors, was getting a little loud. I wondered if we weren't going to get thrown off the premises. Rachel fueled Carla and Nora, and before long we were having a real deliverance service. Soon our quiet little prayer group had strapped on their armor and we were battling in the spirit for the world's largest nation.

I opened a bottle of anointing oil and poured it onto the square as a prophetic act for the remission of sins against the Chinese people by their communist leaders.

After 30 minutes or so we slowly made our way back to our vehicles. I couldn't help but catch a look at a few of the soldiers on our way out. I leaned over to Carla and Nora and said, "Now they know we're all nuts." We nervously chuckled and headed for our hotel.

That first Sunday of 1990 I had the privilege of preaching in one of China's largest Christian churches. This was not an underground house church, but a government sanctioned movement. Pastor Kan, the senior minister, was genuinely friendly and cordial. He really seemed excited that Ron was going to sing "Amazing Grace" for his congregation. This pastor told Nora that I could have 30 minutes to preach on anything I wanted.

Ron sang like, well, only Ron can sing. Then I took the pulpit with my interpreter. I was told that Billy Graham was the only other Christian from the states allowed to have this liberty. *Boy, tough act to follow,* I told myself.

As I looked over the crowd I spotted several men from the secret service, obviously monitoring my message. Instead of teaching, I simply shared my testimony of how I came to Christ. The people laughed and clapped. Many wept.

I prayed that China's people would continue to grow in Christ, and would learn to call upon the Holy Spirit for the power to carry out spiritual warfare.

And Jesus came and spoke to them, saying,
All authority has been given to Me in heaven and on earth.
Go therefore and make disciples of all the nations,
baptizing them in the name of the Father and of the Son and of
the Holy Spirit,
teaching them to observe all things that I have commanded you;
and lo, I am with you always, even to the end of the age. Amen.
—Matthew 28:18-20

CHAPTER 30

Hey, I'm Still Here!

Spiritual warfare doesn't just mean fighting the devil. It means reaping the harvest, celebrating the victory, enjoying the blessings of God.

I turned 50 in 1994. Me—50! Unbelievable, but true. In the Old Testament the year of Jubilee meant the year of release. All debts were forgiven and all slaves were freed. It happened every fifty years. Pentecost also means fifty and in the New Testament represents the outpouring of the Holy Spirit on all flesh— plenty there to be happy about. I'll claim all of this release of forgiveness, praise, and jubilation, in Jesus' name.

1994 began a new spirit of jubilee at our church. My dream team of staff ministers materialized. Dr. Larry and Bette Hayashida, two of the nicest professional people I've ever met, came on staff. My sister Juanita and her husband Ed moved into leadership roles. Jeff and Julie were faithful and talented in the Children's Department. Brian and Pat saw to it our worship experience didn't drop off one iota when Ron Kenoly was on the road, and by now Ron was becoming a legend in the worship world.

A fresh positive feeling infused Jubilee Christian Center.

Crowds soared to the point of having three Sunday morning services and numerous programs and ministeries throughout every week. Our fifteen-member band and lively red-robed choir really rocked in worship and praise. Offerings rose, so that we could begin making plans to finally design a building of our own in a field across the way.

One day in June of 1994, a church member named Carl Story called me and said, "Pastor, meet me at my lawyer's office tomorrow."

"Sure, Carl, what's up?"

Without answering, Carl suggested that I bring Dennis Kim too. The next day we all sat around the lawyer's conference room, when Carl broke into a big smile. "Pastor," he asked, "how do you want the stock made out? To you personally or to the church?" He was talking about 1.5 million shares of a Silicon Valley high tech company getting ready to go on the Nasdaq Board.

"Uh, make it out to Jubilee, Carl." I winked at Dennis. Whew, I passed the temptation test! Shortly afterwards, we sold the stock for 4.2 million dollars. Bless his heart, Carl moved on to find other Christian ministries to help.

Wherever you are, Carl Story, thanks. You were a godsend.

Eye has not seen, nor ear heard,
Nor have entered into the heart of man
The things which God has prepared for those who love Him.
—1 Corinthians 2:9

PART FOUR

THE KINGDOM IS WITHIN

The kingdom of God

does not come with observation;

nor will they say, See here!

or See there!' For indeed,

the kingdom of God is within you.

—Luke 17:20-21

Dick Bernal

CHAPTER 31

A Fresh Look at God the Father

My 50th birthday was special. My best friend Larry Lea came up from Dallas to speak at the church and play golf with me. Oral Roberts preached a Sunday morning service and touched our hearts. My Christian publisher friend Stephen Strang was in town for a visit. Ken Norton, Sr., sent me a pair of boxing gloves with "Happy Birthday" written on each glove. And Merton Hanks— all-pro safety for the 49ers—showed up at my party and gave me a football signed by the Super Bowl championship team of 1994-1995.

They even brought the batmobile up from Los Angeles for me to drive around the hotel parking lot. It was a great time. I felt alive and confident once more. Carla and I were like two high school kids in love. Life was sweet.

While Larry was in town I received a great revelation about my life. As we drove around the golf course, Larry began sharing a recent self-discovery. He said he had lived a shame-based life for many years, always wanting to live up to his earthly father's expectations, yet always falling short. This struck a chord deep within me.

Larry asked, "Dick, ever hear the story of the great London fire a few centuries back?" Matter of fact, I had but the details were sketchy.

Larry proceeded to share about the incident. "During those years there was a horrible black plague that devastated a good part of Europe. No one could figure out what brought it on every spring. And then the worst fire in London's history nearly wiped out the city. It was devastating."

"Spring arrived," Larry continued, "and no plague. Folks were relieved, but puzzled. As the clean-up of the city began, the workers went down into the sewers of London and found piles of dead rats killed by the fire. And millions and millions of dead fleas. The fire killed not only the rats but the plague-carrying fleas."

"Pastor Dick," said Larry, "shame is nothing more than spiritual rats and fleas. The fire of the baptism of the Holy Spirit is the only thing that can get down into the sewers of our souls. God is giving me that fire John the Baptist spoke of and I'm being set free from shame. Pastor Dick, I think you need a dose of Holy Ghost fire yourself."

"Amen, brother," I sighed.

That Friday night as Larry preached at our church I asked God to send the fire. He did! It was painful as the spirit of God went deep down into my life—my past pain, shame, and guilt—and began to burn up the rats and fleas.

As this happened I received a fresh revelation of God as my Father. I had always struggled for a picture of God the Father. I felt more comfortable with Jesus as my Lord. Jesus was a construction worker, so was I. He liked to fish, so did I. He hung out with the boys, so did I. He wasn't afraid of anyone, nor was I. I liked Jesus, and the Holy Spirit was becoming a real friend and helper.

In my prayer time I would talk to Jesus and the Holy Spirit, but felt anxious addressing the Father. *Why get too close to Father God?* I reasoned. *Maybe He too will leave me.* I remember as a seven-year-old waiting for 8 hours out in front of the house for my father to pick me up to go fishing. He had promised the week before, on one of his rare visits, to take me to the lake and teach me how to catch bluegill. He must have gotten drunk or just plain forgot. Nevertheless, I waited and waited. Putting my stuff away in the garage I remember thinking, *Fathers just can't be trusted. Oh well, I still have Grandma, Mom and my sisters. That's enough for me.*

Amazing how young memories last so long. But here I am during my 50th birthday party finally seeing my Heavenly Father in a new way. My real Father. A father to the fatherless, a friend to those in need. The Father dwells within us and it is His good pleasure to give us the kingdom.

Do not fear, little flock,
for it is your Father's good pleasure to give you the kingdom.
—Luke 12:32

CHAPTER 32

My Own Growth

There are times I'll be preaching away, or harping on a particular subject like a prophet out of the Old Testament, and the Lord will whisper, *Dick, you ought to buy your own tape and listen to it yourself.* In fact, one Sunday morning I stopped in the middle of my message and said, "Folks, I'm giving an altar call right now and I'm going to be the first one on my knees asking God for forgiveness."

As I finish this book, I've been thinking over the most important things I've learned in my kingdom journey. What I realized is that most of the truths that have stuck with me have been imparted by other people. This is a kingdom principle in itself. God created us to need each other. And the glue that holds us together is forgiveness and love.

When we commit to grow together in our families, with friends, and as members of our churches, something wonderful happens. We all keep learning about God from one another.

There have been times when my marriage and ministry suffered so much stress that I didn't think I could survive. I lost my vision and my way. The only thing I could think of was people who loved us and were praying. I know Carla sure was. Some-

167

times I've put her through so much that I've wondered why she didn't trade me in on a new model. But Carla can forgive anyone for anything, and she does this for me.

One of the things I've learned from Carla—even though it drives me crazy at times—is that you can pray in the Spirit even in awful moments. Time and again I've seen her do this. She finds the joy of victory in her heart while I'm still sitting on the pity pot.

Pastor Cho has taught me that you can pastor the largest church and still doubt yourself and wonder about your calling. David Yonggi Cho is the most transparent minister that I've ever known. He has the rare ability to tell what a flop he is and be cheered by his congregation for his realness. I hope that I am learning to do the same.

I admire Jack Hayford, pastor of The Church on the Way, because he shows that you can have a little bit of intelligence and still be a Pentecostal. Too often in the past those dear souls who had the Pentecostal fire put down higher education. But ole Jack is so educated that I need to take a dictionary to his meetings to look up what he's saying, so I can say "amen."

Robert Schuller of Crystal Cathedral told me to be myself no matter how much pressure there is to conform to others. Schuller took a lot of flack for his positive thinking approach, but really he was just putting the Gospel in positive terms. Millions are blessed because he stuck with it.

From that precious saint of God, Oral Roberts, I've learned how to be strong as horseradish and yet have people still love me. Oral is the strongest man I've ever been around, yet he is sweet as a rose. He'll tell you the truth even if he knows you won't like it. He needed that strength of character to confront all the powerful diseases he came against. In my book, Oral Roberts is a man's man.

Lester Sumrall has taught me that a man with a vision doesn't have time to die until he's finished the course. At the age of 83, Dr. Sumrall recently finished his course and went on to be with the Lord. What an inspiration he was to me.

The troops at Jubilee Christian Center show me that you

can't box God into a corner. These wonderful people come from all walks of life, economic ranges, and ethnic backgrounds. Yet the love and grace of God is extremely evident among them, and this fact inspires me when I get in the valley. My congregation teaches me that God is colorful, adventurous, humorous, and creative.

And, Dick Bernal? What do I have to teach anyone? Maybe that you can get knocked down without being knocked out. You can always get up and try again.

My Christian life has been a lot like learning how to water ski. A friend took me out on a beautiful lake one day. I was convinced that I'd be up on those blasted skis the first try. But after two hours of pulling, tugging, and fighting the rope, my arms were almost out of sockets and I had gulped down part of the lake.

My friend, in a voice reminiscent of the Lord, finally said, "Dick, if you'll just relax and let the boat pull you, everything will be okay." So I gave up and relaxed, and what do you know? A few seconds later I was skiing like a champ.

What I like about the Lord is that whether we're quick studies or relatively dumb, whether we grew up as saints from the crib or played craps for most of our lives, when we enter the kingdom of God, we become His children. And no matter what blows the devil dishes out or what Jesus asks us to do, we can rest assured that the kingdom of God is within us.

I close with a picture of my latest catastrophe, which my dear wife is already claiming as a great victory for Jesus. We're days from breaking ground for our new building with a sanctuary that will seat 3,500. The troops are fired up and yours truly is gung-ho, when I get a call saying that the army corps of engineers wants to turn our building site into a marsh for ducks.

I slam down my home phone and feel a pounding headache coming on. I hustle out the front door to drive to my office, gearing up for battle with the devil and the U.S. government. I take just long enough to grumble about the problem on the way out the door, but my wife clearly grasps the situation and begins dancing and praying in the Spirit.

I rev up my black GMC Jimmy and get ready to put the pedal to the metal. Just then Carla comes running out of our home in this nice respectable neighborhood, wearing her white terry cloth bathrobe, waving her arms, and declaring to the world, "Dick, everything is okay! Honey, the battle is the Lord's—and He's already won."

And you know what? She's right!

> *For the battle is the LORD'S,*
> *and He will give you into our hands.*
> *—1Samuel 17:47*

OTHER BOOKS BY DICK BERNAL

•**Lifting Him Up (By Dick Bernal and Ron Kenoly)**

•**Removing the "Ites" From Your Promised Land**

•**America Spiritually Mapped**

•**When Lucifer and Jezebel Join Your Church**

•**Questions God Asks**

•**Who is God? What is Man?**

•**Curses: What They Are and How to Break Them**

•**Come Down Dark Prince**

For a complete listing of our audio and video tape collection
call or write to:

Jubilee Christian Center
175 Nortech Parkway
San Jose, California 95134
(408)262-0900

Dick Bernal